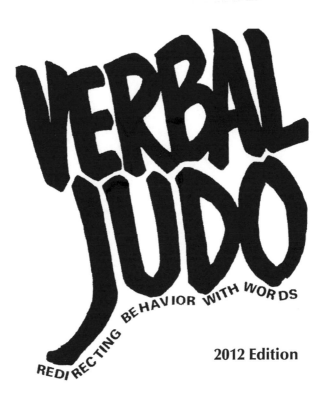

VERBAL JUDO

REDIRECTING BEHAVIOR WITH WORDS

2012 Edition

VERBAL
JUDO

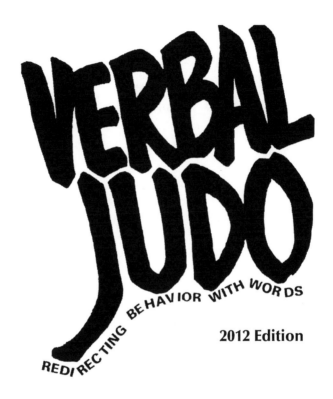

2012 Edition

George J. Thompson, Ph.D

Published by

The Verbal Judo Institute, Inc. • www.verbaljudoglobal.com

Verbal Judo: Redirecting Behavior with Words
By George J. Thompson, Ph.D.

2012 Edition

Copyright 2012:
        The Verbal Judo Institute, Inc.
        http://www.verbaljudoglobal.com

International Standard Book Number: 978-0-9885562-0-1

First printing 1984. Second Printing 1994.

Production for publisher done by Word Productions and
Sherwood Printing LLC.

Published by:
The Verbal Judo Institute, Inc.
http://www.verbaljudoglobal.com

Dedication

Verbal Judo as a program and the Verbal Judo Institute, Inc., as a company, are alive and well in the United States and reaching around the world. From our hearts to yours, a short history behind this publication and our purpose as a company. George J. Thompson, a tenured collegiate professor turned cop, then turned professional trainer launched a personal mission—that a dedicated team of people can bring a message which will save careers, reduce burn out, and reduce stress, if we could just communicate better.

At first police didn't embrace the idea of words as a legitimate force option, considering it common sense where each officer must work from his or her own gifts and experience. Thompson believed the professional use of language under stressful conditions could indeed be taught and so he charged at skeptical audiences relentlessly, and as one participant commented, "Like a rhinoceros on amphetamines!"

Thompson's words found an audience, his tactics and strategies proving time and time again we don't need to become angered at difficult people and stressful situations. Using a tactical form of civility for focusing on behavior, not people's attitudes, we can learn to redirect the actions and the language of others during conflict.

Verbal Judo expanded quickly outside of law enforcement into the world of business, airlines, the cruise industries, the medical profession, education, and became hugely popular with government employees in city, county and federal offices. Verbal Judo is also recognized by general audiences for helping parents and children deal with the damaging effects of bullying. An upcoming book co-authored by George's wife, Pam Thompson will be released in the near future.

George Thompson began this endeavor as a business in 1984, forming the Verbal Judo Institute, Inc., expanding the reach of his noble pursuit with his first associate in 1985. Followed by others dedicated to teaching his principles over the next two decades Verbal Judo flourished.   Since the mid-eighties over one million people have sat in Verbal Judo classes and hundreds of thousands more have read Thompson's books, watched the videos, and listen to the audio versions of Verbal Judo.

The sad passing in 2011 of Dr. George J. Thompson III, aka Rhino, has left a hole in our hearts, but his legacy and his original program will move forward - We promise.

From W. Lee Fjelstad and Pam Thompson

And from the rest of our Verbal Judo family in the United States: Mike Manley, Doug Haig, Steve Wopershall; and from William King in Australia, Darcy Pennock in Canada, Bo Munthe in Sweden, and Don Gold in South Africa.

In Memory of Dr. George "Doc" Thompson, aka Rhino

How to Read This Book and Why

This is the third printing of Verbal Judo: Redirecting Behavior with Words and sadly, Dr. Thompson will not be here to autograph the copies, or speak in front of the audiences he came to believe were his legacy. The passing of my friend and mentor has left me the heavyhearted duty of updating his work. Rather than editing in changes to make the book more readily connected to life twenty-seven years after its first printing, we at the Verbal Judo Institute have chosen another route. The book will remain in its original format. We rather you as the reader see this book as George originally scripted it.

It is important to note the central tenant of Verbal Judo is all people deserve to be treated with respect, to have their opinions and needs addressed or at least acknowledged, and to be treated fairly. George Thompson always believed in his heart the necessity of preserving dignity while Generating Voluntary Compliance from others as a professional purpose. Wherever minds are in discord we need an action plan and an effective way to implement it.

The tactics in Verbal Judo have universal applicability; they can be used to deal with any person under almost any type of conditions. Although no one can guarantee an absolute result, Verbal Judo strategies offer a better prospect for getting what you need than any other working set of principles I have ever used. Redirecting Behavior with Words is the second book in the Verbal Judo collection "penned" by Dr. Thompson. Yes, penned, because it was first written in longhand with pen and ink, a painstaking process considering the almost effortless use of a computer today. Therefore, this book and its predecessor, Words as a Force Option were both a labor of heart and a mission to the ultimate goal of reducing verbal violence in our world.

Please read the lessons carefully and reapply the examples offered in these pages to your own "situational rhetoric". Use words to change not only the behavior of others but to modify how you see and approach conflict. Use words to help bring about change for a better society, one infused with less scorn for adversarial situations.

A picture is worth a thousand words. No one truly knows who first stated this truism but the fact remains that stories –the ones that actually stay on point—demonstrate we can learn from the dealings of others to improve our own lives measurably. Imagery creates the picture in our mind as we are projected into the scene as an observer. I was once told that true artistry is in making the difficult look easy. So, if a story can take complicated rhetorical strategies used by Aristotle over 2,000 years ago to segue into dealing with disagreeable people today, we should take note.

We should certainly also apply these principles to achieve one of George Thompson's most known maxims, "Think for others as they would think for themselves after the influence has worn off." From emotional outbursts to self-indulging attitudes to the instant gratification of our modern techno society can be overcome if we can use empathy—to see through the eyes of the other and "leave others better than we found them at their worst". If we can employ verbal strategies to get what we need without demeaning others, we will advance society and embrace humanity more than in all recorded history.

Each chapter was written as a progression with a challenge, an encounter, and finally a lesson learned. The Challenge is life. The Encounter is found in every aspect of human interaction, and the Lesson is often a simple golden rule that we have all learned but perhaps forget when we are tired, stressed, or thinking; I'm just not taking any crap today! In an upcoming book I will address a phrase I learned long ago in Zen meditation from a monk I met during my travels. It goes something like this, "If others hurt more, will you hurt less?"

The profundity is in our own ability to acknowledge our own temperament and adapt.

W. Lee Fjelstad, Vice President of the Verbal Judo Institute, Inc.

In memory of Dr. George J. Thompson III - his work, his teachings, his writings, and his legacy

The Second Printing Preface written in 1994 by Dr. George J. Thompson III, Ph.D., in 1994

I first published this book in 1984. I thought at the time the dramatic scenes described would help readers see the general applicability of Verbal Judo (or Tactical Communication, as it is sometimes called) in one's daily life.

I still believe this to be true of the scene depicted, but I now know after twenty-five plus years of using the book as an accompaniment to my professional training that it holds even greater power than I first thought—but only if it is used correctly.

Only when a student surpasses his Master has the Master truly taught his Art. So I say "thank you" to the thousands of students over the years who have sharpened my sense of the potential value of this little handbook, Hence this revision and new introduction.

Although people learn in different ways, many learn best through "stories" or examples of principles in action. I try to teach here not by lecture or discussion but by example, letting the real event speak for itself.

Each story is factually true; I depict the events as they happened to me. I only fictionalize the names of the participants. I let other "characters" play my various roles in the stories because I want to play narrator and commentator on the action.

Each story illustrates a single kind of language in action—the Language of Reassurance, the Language of Motivation or the Language of Punishment, and the point of each story is the Principle itself. The principles need to be memorized, not the stories.

Unlike most "how-to" books, this little book does not provide the "how" so much as the "what." If an officer or reader can remember, for example that if he or she has to reassure people before redirecting their behavior, he or she must project empathy (understanding) in word and deed. How he does this is individual and various—there may be hundreds of ways to do it—but it must be done or the audience will not calm down.

People who work with the public in the difficult arenas of changing or modifying behavior must be able to act quickly and effectively. Memorize these eight Principles of language, for they will markedly aid you in finding the right verbal responses under pressure.

Persuasion is an art, a craft, and a "way" of life for many of us. This little book can go a long way towards giving you the power of influence others lack.

VERBAL
JUDO

Prologue

The Lesson of the Willow

Verbal Judo is a series of tactics based on the principles of nonresistance. Rather than confront another's antagonism, Verbal Judo teaches us to turn aggressiveness aside and to use the other's energies to achieve positive goals.

While the tactics of Verbal Judo may seem new, the underlying principle of nonresistance was first stated almost 1,300 years ago. According to legend, a Japanese physician named Shirobei Akiyama discovered that precept during a retreat at the temple of Tenji.

Dr. Akiyama had entered the temple after an extensive stay in China. There he had studied Taoism, and had accepted the ethical principles of that philosophy— principles that stressed quietism, balance, and equilibrium with the world around.

Now he was deeply troubled by an apparent contradiction between his beliefs and his experience. While the doctrine of peaceful balance appealed to him, he could not apply it to situations of conflict and strife. Again and again he struggled with the problem:

How can such a lesson apply to my people? We are a small nation, easily overwhelmed by superior force. The principles of the Tao would lead to our destruction, for how can any aggression be defeated, save through even greater aggressiveness? How can the Tao help us defeat a superior force?

During each of the 100 days of his retreat, Dr. Akiyama walked through the nearby woods, wrestling with his dilemma. Each day he sought the answer by interpreting the natural events he observed.

Near the end of his stay at Tenji, he walked along his familiar path, now transformed by a heavy snowfall, and stopped before a large willow tree. At his feet, the doctor noticed numerous broken branches, still encased in sleeves of ice and snow. Above him, however, all was different. Many of the willow's wands, free of any covering, swayed gently in the chili breeze. He sensed that the scene before him somehow contained the answer he sought:

Nature is the most powerful of opponents. No one can conquer it. Victory over such an enemy can mean only continued survival, not triumph.

Dr. Akiyama shuddered as a clump of wet snow fell on his unprotected neck. He looked up to see a willow branch whip into the sky. At once he knew that he had found his answer:

Now I see! These branches that lay broken before me were strong and resolute. They stood firm and resisted the opposing forces of nature. When the wet snow fell on them, they bore the weight without flinching.

While their resistance seems heroic, it was self-destructive. For when the enemy is inexorable, as is the snow, these strong branches are doomed by the weight that accumulates—accumulates until they break beneath it.

But these wands that sway above me are delicate and supple. They cannot resist. They give way to their opponent, nature, and shed their killing burden. The weaker combatant survives—and thus wins—by turning force aside, rather than by resisting.

And so must be the ways of nations and those in personal combat. No resistance can ever defeat a superior force. Only suppleness will lead to true victory.

The lesson read in nature that snowy day was to become a new doctrine. Dr. Akiyama opened a school that remained in existence for centuries. He named it yoshinryu, "the heart of the willow". There he adapted ancient principles of unarmed combat—principles from India, China, and other nations—to create the art of jujitsu.

Dr. Akiyama's simple truth has endured for 13 centuries. Each new era has reinterpreted that lesson in response to new opponents and unforeseen sources of aggression. The most recent revision led to the art of Judo, begun in 1882 by Dr. Jigoro Kano, an educator who had studied at Oxford. Verbal Judo is but a new application of the willow's truth.

The principles of Verbal Judo are based on the principles of physical judo, and some of the tactics of Verbal Judo parallel those of physical judo. The descriptions of the physical tactics in each chapter, however, are intended to enhance understanding of the verbal techniques, not to teach the art of judo.

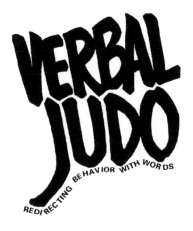

CONTENTS

VERBAL
JUDO

1

The Limits of Force

The Need for Verbal Judo

"Fourteen hours across the desert," Mike said to himself as the car rushed along Interstate 40, "A chance to catch up on my reverie."

From the passenger seat of the speeding car, he could see the high New Mexico desert extend for miles. In his mind he joined earlier travelers in their journeys across the desert—Mark Twain from the east and Hunter Thompson from the west.

His destination was Las Vegas, the same city immortalized in the accounts of Gonzo Journalism. A curious combination of circumstances had sent him and the driver—George—on this 600-mile drive across the American desert to Las Vegas. They were going to work, not to gamble or observe.

As the miles passed, Mike found himself increasingly bored with his thoughts. George's words interrupted the

silence: "By my calculations, we'll be there in just 12 hours and 45 minutes."

"That long?" Mike marveled. "Guess we better find something to do."

"I've been struggling with Verbal Judo, George responded. "Why don't you help me work?"

"I'll talk to you about it," Mike answered, "but I can't say I'm optimistic. I love the phrase --Verbal Judo—it's really catchy. But what else do you have? Is it a fighting tactic, some mysterious art, or just a gift of gab? Ancient fighting tactics don't seem to solve the kinds of problems our clients have."

"I think you watched Kung Fu too many times," George said with a laugh. "You think of judo as some deep secret hidden away in a temple on a mountain. In fact, judo is fairly recent and very scientific.

"About a hundred years ago, a Japanese educator named Jigoro Kano went to Oxford, where he studied anatomy. After reading the texts, he concluded that jujitsu—a truly ancient art—could actually hurt the martial artist because of the stress some moves put on the muscle structure. So he changed some moves and invented new ones, taking better advantage of human anatomy and the laws of physics. And he devised a series of ethical maxims as well, so that his new martial art—judo—would also be a way of life as well.

"What I've been trying to do over the past couple of months is to use those principles to create a new way to respond to aggression. Judo for our time."

"I'm not disagreeing with that goal," Mike answered energetically. "When you look out at this desert, there doesn't seem to be an urgent need for Verbal Judo. But even out here, sparse as the population is, people rub up against each other all the time; out east it's impossible. Americans are going to have to give up their frontier ideals in order to live together. There isn't open land enough for our old role models—gunslingers and mountain men.

"But," he went on, "how can any form of judo change those problems? Isn't judo just another culture's form of aggressiveness?"

George's eyes left the road momentarily as he looked at his companion. "My friend, don't you know that judo is the gentle art? The name itself comes from two Japanese words: ju means 'gentle' or 'soft', and do means 'way'. And it is an art, one that perfects the individual. The etiquette and physical training of judo develop self-control, humility, and resolve—the very qualities contribute to a higher degree of social order."

"I appreciate that perspective," Mike replied, "because it's different from mine. I see kids lined up outside movie houses showing martial arts films, and I'm very sure they aren't looking forward to an exercise of gentle arts. And sometimes, when I get back real late from a trip, I'll turn on the television to relax. The cable sports channels have lots of 'full-contact' karate and kick boxing and the like. I know you see an ethic in the martial arts, but I don't think most Americans do."

"I'll admit I would like to change that popular image," George said, "and Verbal Judo may be a way to do it. At least you agree with me that some change has to take place in the way people get along with each other.

"This society has lots of different forms of violence. People hurt each other in unnumbered ways. The most aggressive and the most hurtful attacks can't be countered with the skills I learned in my studies of martial arts.

"Children act abusively toward their parents, employees and employers ridicule each other, customers and salespeople insult one another. If a man pushes ahead of me in a line, I can't use a foot sweep to punish that aggressiveness. This society does not allow physical attacks. Think of it—burglars sue homeowners when they're hurt during a break-in.

"We need Verbal Judo," he said forcefully, "a way that people can respond to aggression with words, not physical strength."

"Sure," Mike responded with a hint of cynicism. "But when I was growing up, kids used to sing a song:

Sticks and stones

May break my bones,

But words,

Can never hurt me.

"If someone was coming after you with a stick, you'd protect yourself with more than words. And so would most people. Words are a civilized way to disagree, but not everyone is civilized."

"Of course not," George answered seriously, "but be careful not to reject this idea without examining it. My judo master used to tell stories about a lazy doctor from the town where he spent his childhood. The doctor didn't bother to examine people to diagnose. When patients came to see him he demanded to know 'What is your disease? What treatment do you need?' You want to say it won't work because you can't see how it will work."

"I'm not denying your point," Mike said, a bit defensively. "Being good with words is always better than not being good with words. But why drag in judo?"

"I don't think I'm 'dragging' it in," replied George. "Dr. Kano, the man who invented judo, had a principle he called seiryoku zenryo. That principle tells us how to use our energy effectively, attaining maximum efficiency with minimum effort. As I see it, that should be the goal in using words."

"You win again," Mike answered. "But why not call it 'Verbal Karate'? You're an expert in more than one of these disciplines."

"There's an important difference here," George answered thoughtfully. "Judo is very different from karate and other 'attacking' techniques. Judo is a 'grappling' art; you must never lose contact with the 'other' if you're to move him with skill. It is a 'hand-to-hand' art, one of parrying, deflecting, and countering. It is an art for responding to others' energy rather than attacking. It cannot be used at a distance.

"And that," he concluded, "makes judo a good metaphor for the use of words I'm talking about."

"I feel persuaded. Is that Verbal Judo at work?" Mike laughed. "Aren't you concerned, though, that other martial arts experts may resent your manipulation of their principles of combat?"

"I certainly don't want any Black Belts looking for me," George said sincerely. "But I don't feel I'm 'manipulating' anything. The principles of judo—non-resistance and countering—aren't changeable, and they aren't related only to combat. The tactics, on the other hand, have changed constantly. Dr. Kano developed new tactics because of his research. His son carried his work on, revising techniques based on scientific research.

"And really, that's all I'm doing, adapting the principles of judo to this time and culture."

"But isn't this just the 'gift of gab'?" challenged Mike. "My sense of judo is that it uses very specific tactics and moves. Is there anything like that in Verbal Judo?"

"That's why I need your help," George responded. "I've got some of the principles clear now, but I need to relate them to specific types of actions. I do know, however, that people can improve. I learned how to use words better during my life, and I've seen other people get better. We must be talking about something that can be learned, not a natural talent."

"I'm a believer," Mike answered. "But who's going to teach us this art? Didn't you have a Master when you studied different martial arts?"

"You're right about that," answered George. "I suppose that we have to look for answers the way Dr. Akiyama did, by observing nature."

"I think we should observe people, instead," Mike said. "I don't think the desert has any answers to this problem."

"Agreed," answered George. "Whom do we observe?"

"Let's try to figure that out after breakfast," Mike answered. "I'm starving. Gallup is ahead. Let's eat, then I'll drive and we can figure out who our 'experts' will be."

VERBAL
JUDO

2

The Language of Guidance

The Challenge

"Two orders of biscuits and gravy for breakfast," Mike said in astonishment as he pulled away from the parking lot. "I don't know how you do it."

They reentered the highway heading west, with Mike now driving. George tilted the passenger seat back and asked, "So, any ideas about where we'll find our Verbal Judo expert?"

"How could I know?" asked Mike. "This is your theory, not mine."

"That's true," said George "but you're the one who works with people who have visible, public jobs. I'm sure you've met some who were good with words, and who could explain what they tried to do, even if they didn't call it Verbal Judo."

"I don't see the same kinds of confrontations that you do, George," Mike responded, "so I only hear second-hand reports. I can't really judge how successfully situations have been handled." He paused for a moment, then smiled. "I will grant that some second-hand reports are better than others. For example, there's Shirley Martinez."

"Tell me about her," said George.

"Shirley Martinez is an enforcement officer from the state Department of Environmental Protection," Mike answered. "I've worked with her preparing a few Environmental Impact Statements. She has one of the tough jobs."

"You talk," George said. "I'll write up your observations."

The Encounter

Late one afternoon a few years before, Mike had sat in a straight-back chair of steel and vinyl waiting for an appointment with Mrs. Shirley Martinez. The room in which he sat was immense, but all the available space had been sectioned off into cubicles for working. The steal walls that created the squares scarcely reached his six-foot height, and he could easily have looked into Mrs. Martinez's area had he stood.

As he waited, he found himself reading the posters and slogans celebrating nature's orderly cycle. Most of the cubicles were empty; only the erratic tapping of a manual typewriter across the room and the continuous ringing of phones broke the institutional stillness.

Mike gradually discovered that he had unconsciously begun to listen in on a nearby conversation. Despite his innate respect for others' privacy, he could not help listening, and he felt trapped—like a schizophrenic, he thought, who cannot ignore the voices that speak to him from within.

"Mom," the youthful voice said plaintively, "I can't get a ride to the game and I'm going to miss it again. I just have to get a car."

"I understand how frustrating it can be to try and scare up a ride, Lee," a woman's voice responded. "A car would solve a lot of your problems. You just want to be sure you don't create even more problems for yourself."

"What do you mean?" the boy responded.

"Well, for one, how will you pay for it?"

The room was momentarily silent. "Couldn't you and Dad buy one for me?"

"We would certainly like to, but I can't promise when we'll be able to do that."

"But I need it now!"

"I understand that, Lee, and if there were any way to do it now, we would. But you've looked at the budget with your father and me, and you know that there isn't much left over after the basic bills are paid."

"It isn't fair," the youthful voice responded, almost cracking. "Jim Weir's parents bought him one."

"Jim's parents come from a wealthy background and they have more money to solve this kind of problem with than your father and I do. I know it isn't 'fair', and I wish that we had more, but I can't do anything to change it."

"How about if I take some of my college savings to buy the car? I know that I could get a job delivering groceries for Kaune's Market and earn it all back before I start college."

"You could probably do that, Lee. But do you remember what happens to the 'best laid plans'? If you use all your college money to buy a car, and something goes wrong…"

"Nothing will go wrong," the boy's voice returned.

"Of course not. But just in case something does happen, you have to protect yourself from that chance of disaster. That's why we spend so much on insurance—for the 'just in case' part of life."

"But what if I only take out $500? That would leave enough to start the first year at school."

"That makes sense to me, as long as you can stay under $500," she responded.

"I'm sure I can," he answered. "Jim's cost $650. I can find something cheaper.

"Let me make a suggestion," she said. "I'm sure you know that you'll have some expenses when you buy the car. Why don't you total up those expenses and see how much you have left to actually spend on the car itself?"

"How much do you think those things will cost?" he asked.

"I honestly don't know. Why don't you check with Jim?"

"Be back soon," the boy's voice said. Mike looked up as a tall youth rushed past, but the young man did not look at him.

"I'm sorry to keep you waiting. Won't you come in?" He looked in the direction of the voice he had just overheard. "It's good to see you again," she smiled. "You must have seen my son leaving."

"He's a good-looking boy," Mike responded.

Mrs. Martinez appeared much as she had during her visits to a remote mining site when they had worked together, except that she wore a light knit vest instead of a bulky down jacket. She was probably in her early 40's and her complexion revealed both the benefit of outdoor work and the cost.

"What can I do for you?" she asked cheerfully as he followed her into the small cubicle.

"I've come to you for some help," he began. "Do you recall the citation your department issued to a man named David Ackerman? It had something to do with the sewage system on his ranch."

"I think so," she replied. "As I recall, his system was polluting a stream that ran through his property."

"I've known him for several years. Your notice, plus the first estimate he got from the contractor, made him angrier than anyone had ever seen before. And yet, after your call, he made the changes willingly.

"Well," he continued, "one of my clients from another state was recently cited for operating a plant in violation of the local air-quality standards. I know that isn't your specialization, but I'm trying to persuade them to comply rather than to resist in court, and I could use some help. Will you tell me your secret that allowed you to turn someone like Dave around?"

I don't think I have a secret," she said with a smile, "but I have had to think about ways to guide people since I've come to work here.

"My job, as you probably know," she went on, "is to check sanitation systems in rural parts of the state. It isn't very romantic work, but it keeps the streams and rivers clean.

"The situation up at the Ackerman ranch was as typical as these things get. He had an old system that relied on a cesspool. Cesspools were the state of the art just 25 years ago. Now, we know better.

"It had to be replaced. When I got there, I saw an obvious health hazard and a clear violation of the law. Sometimes, the facts speak for themselves.

"But that isn't what Mr. Ackerman saw, and that isn't what any of the citizens I meet see. Your friend put in that system back in the '30's, and he was upset that he would have to make changes. But many of the people in the far northern part of the state have used the same type of system for eight and ten generations.

"Think how long that is." She paused while he thought. "And here I come, telling them they're breaking the law. Not much chance of instant compliance there."

"But it is true, isn't it, that if the law has been broken, you can force people to make the changes?"

"I sure could," she answered firmly. "My department almost never loses one of these cases. But it takes forever, and costs a fortune, and the press gets involved, and everybody gets angry. Besides, I want to save rivers and wildlife, not wait around outside a courtroom.

"So, I've tried to develop ways to convince people to do the right thing."

"Will you tell me what you do?" he asked. "I'm searching for such a tactic."

"It isn't too complicated. I think I learned it from my mother. She ran a ranch in Texas by herself, and she had to get great big cowboys to do what had to be done. She always said, 'You can reason with anybody as long as you know their reasons.'

"And I guess that's what I do, reason with them. However misinformed and wrongheaded they may be by every standard of reasonableness and good sense—and they can be pretty wrongheaded—I talk to them from their point of reasoning."

"Mom, can I talk to you for a moment?" Mike looked over his shoulder at the boy he had seen earlier.

"Lee, this is a business associate of mine," she said, glancing at Mike. "I don't think he'll mind if I spend a minute with you." Mrs. Martinez left the small work area, but Mike could still hear their conversation very clearly.

"Jim showed me a whole stack of things about taxes and registration and a couple other things," the boy said in a hurt voice. "It's terrible. I'll only have about $400 to spend on the car."

"I hope that will be enough," she said sympathetically.

"Oh, yeah," he went on. "I'll also need to put the car on your insurance policy."

"I don't think we can afford that," she answered.

"But you already have insurance. Why can't you just add another car?'

"Every car has to be paid for separately," she responded. "That's how insurance companies work."

"Jim's insurance costs him almost $150 every six months. I'll only have $250 left over. How can I get anything with that?"

"I don't know," she said with concern. "Why don't you go back to the beginning of your problem to see if you've looked at all the possibilities?"

"My problem is that I need a car," he said angrily.

"Not exactly, Lee. You can use one of the family cars in the evenings. Your problem has to do with days like today, when the game begins in the afternoon. You need to decide how much you can spend to solve it. Why don't you think it through again? There might be a solution you haven't considered."

"I still don't think it's fair," he answered.

"I know, darling. I'll be happy to do some brainstorming with you tonight."

"Maybe I should get a 10-speed," he said. "Anyway, I'm going to ride up with Jim to see the rest of the game. See you tonight."

"Let's talk about it later. I'll see you at home," she said.

"Please excuse the interruption," she said as she returned to her desk. "Weren't we just talking about trying to guide people to take the right action? I'm sure you couldn't help overhearing my conversation with my son. I try to use the same kind of reasoning with him as I do in my work.

"As I'm sure you heard; he wants a car. To him, that's a complete and reasoned decision. His reasoning is not so different from the guy I ran into yesterday who told me his sewage system's sound because his great-grandfather built it. He and my son both think they have all the evidence they need to make a good decision.

"If I say 'You don't have all the evidence you need', do you think they'll listen to me? If I say 'What you're doing is reckless', do you think they'll suddenly see the fallacy of their logic and say 'you're right'?"

Mike smiled. "I'm sure not," he said.

"People who are unreasonable don't know that they're unreasonable, and that's true whether they're teenagers or adults. When people think they're being reasonable, you can't attack their conclusions. You have to guide them to a better conclusion using their reasoning.

"My son, for example, wants a car. It isn't a reasonable or an achievable want, according to my reasoning.

Circumstances prohibit him from getting a car. He hasn't the money to buy one, let alone repair one, and he doesn't know how to keep an old clunker running.

"That's the reasoning process that I'm using. I don't want to say that I never make mistakes, though I'm pretty confident that I'm right in this situation. But no matter how sure I am, or even how right I might be, I know two things: first, that he isn't using my reasoning process, and second, that he's as sure of his reasoning process and his conclusions as I am of mine.

"So, if I tell him 'No, you can't buy a car, that's unreasonable', then no matter how good my reasons are, all he'll hear is me denying his ability to reason.

"So what will happen is that he'll get angry and blame me for being unreasonable rather than recognize that the circumstances prevent him from getting that car. And he'll take out all his frustrations about those unavoidable circumstances in a fight with me, rather than learn the painful lesson that says 'you can't always get what you want'."

He smiled at the phrase. "I can see why you might think my friend acted like a teenager. But is it wise to treat adults like children?"

"I would say instead that I treat teenagers like adults and reason with them rather than get angry. When Lee came in and demanded a car, I felt quite irritated. He knows money is tight now, and that I can't do anything about his problem.

"But I can't reason with him if I express that anger and say, in effect, 'How can you be so unreasonable? Why don't you know what I know about life?' I want to help him reach a more mature perspective.

"So I didn't say 'no' when he first brought it up. I agreed with him and then showed him the next step in his own reasoning.

"And when he talked about using his college savings, I had to restrain myself from saying 'Don't be ridiculous. What about your future?' I have to validate his reasoning before changing his mind.

"His plan to buy a car with his college money and earn the money back later isn't completely foolish; it just ignores 'Murphy's Law'."

"You mean that something will go wrong?"Mike asked.

"More like 'if something can go wrong, it will'. But even more important, you can't know what can go wrong until it goes wrong. And if you don't have lots of backup in place for things going wrong, your plan falls through.

"Lee's attitude is a lot like some of the uranium-mining companies I have to work with. They get the best designers in the country and draw up a perfectly engineered solution to their tailings disposal problem. And I have to reject it, because it has no natural backup for that engineering solution—no anticipation of Murphy's Law.

"But if I state my feelings—whether to the Chief Engineer at a mine, or to my son—I make myself less effective. I have to control my frustration at their unreasonableness, accept the fact that they think they're reasonable, and reason with them."

He heard a youthful voice over his shoulder demanding Mrs. Martinez's attention: "Shirley, did you say Lee could get a car?"

"Rick, I'm busy right now," the woman answered.

"I'm sorry, but it is after 5:00," the boy replied.

"You're right. I apologize for working late."

Mike smiled at her words and looked at the youth. He was struck that this boy, larger and of darker complexion, had to be the same age as the boy he had seen earlier.

"Did you say that Lee could get a car?" he asked again.

"He has been thinking about it, Rick. You should talk to him about what he's learned."

"If he gets to get a car, I'm going to get one too," he said in a burst of words as he bounded from the doorway.

"Another son?" he asked.

"My husband's son from a previous marriage," she answered. "We're raising the two of them."

"Do you find your reasoning technique works with him?" he asked.

"Nearly as well, but natural parents do have an advantage. It's a lot like the difference between me and uniformed police officers. We both enforce, but their uniforms and badges tell everybody who they are. I have to spend a lot more time establishing credibility than a policeman or his father does."

He could sense the darkness growing outside the office building. "I'm keeping you late at your desk," he said. "Thank you for your time. You have helped me immensely."

"You're welcome," she said, rising from her chair. "I guess it really comes down to what you use your words for. You can use them to express how you feel or you can use words that will help others reason better."

The Lesson

"You're smiling," Mike said. "Do you know Mrs. Martinez's secret?"

"I believe I understand how she succeeds," answered George, "but there's no secret. In every encounter, she strives to understand the other's point of view and to reason from that point."

"How can that be a new tactic? Don't many people try to understand their opponent?"

"Most people believe they do," George answered, "but few control their feelings when the other's view offends their sense of reason. If we want to view the world through another's eyes, we must see the situation as they see it. We can't judge the rightness or wrongness of their perceptions."

"Does that mean that there is no right or wrong in these things?" Mike asked.

"There is a right action for Mrs. Martinez. She seeks to enforce laws that she feels are right, and she seeks to raise her children to become successful, independent adults."

"So her use of words has a socially useful purpose," Mike concluded. "That fits in with your explanation of judo."

"Let me explain it even further," George said with animation. "Her principle is a lot like Dr. J. Kano's First Maxim of Judo, Jiko no kansei. Dr. Kano taught that each individual must constantly strive for greater perfection.

"Mrs. Martinez uses words to achieve jiko no kansei. She becomes more perfect in her role as mother and government official through her use of words. She uses language to fulfill social responsibility, not to express her own feelings."

"And because she works for mutual benefit," Mike interrupted, "she also helps those she talks with. She helps people make better decisions, decisions to their benefit and to their society's benefit."

"I believe, my friend," George added, "that we have found our First Maxim of Verbal Judo."

Move confrontations away from conclusions back to the reasoning process.

"I like it," Mike responded. "But one thing still bothers me."

"Tell me later. The next exit is for Winslow, and I've wanted to see it for a long time. Let's stop."

3

The Language of Motivation

The Challenge

"I never understood before how sad that old song by the Eagles was," Mike said as they reentered the highway after exchanging roles. "I wouldn't want to be standing on any corner in Winslow, waiting for a ride."

"I feel a bit guilty whenever we pass by one of these hitchhikers," George said from the driver's seat. "At least I feel positive about Verbal Judo as a principle for action."

"Well," Mike responded, "I'm still a bit concerned about generalizing too much from Mrs. Martinez's experience."

"Why?" George asked. "I thought that we were getting our principles in order. Our adaptation of Dr. Kano's jiko no kansei appeals to me."

"Don't forget that we like what Mrs. Martinez does," Mike returned, "and we may tend to justify her means by her goals. But some people do use martial arts to bully people. Our principle seems to say that people should always calculate their words. A maxim like that can lead to glibness, and even justify the tactics of a 'confidence man'—someone who doesn't believe in anything.

"So," he concluded, "I do see a risk in Verbal Judo. It's morally neutral and that can lead to exploitation."

"Well, I don't think that's the outcome if you keep following Dr. Kano's principles," George said. "He talked a good deal about the social consequences of judo. He stressed the importance of cooperation and mutual benefit, arguing that each person's contribution makes the sum of a society greater than its parts. That means all of us have to strive for perfection as individuals to perfect one another, even as we strive to perfect one another."

"But doesn't a problem come up in the translation from the Japanese?" Mike asked. "Japan's a homogenous culture. When you say that everyone should strive for a common social goal, everyone shares a similar sense of what's good for society. But, society here in America is marked by its diversity. It's hard to say what common goals everyone should strive for."

"You can make things tough," George said. "But you're right. The problem is tricky. On one side, Verbal Judo has to have some ethical base—to keep it from becoming exploitive."

"Right."

"And, at the other extreme, Verbal Judo can't simply preach our values—or anyone else's, for that matter," George concluded.

"That's the problem. Do you have an answer?"

"No and yes," George responded, "No, in the sense that any skill or ability can be turned to bad purposes. Yes, because there is an ethic in Verbal Judo that fits your test."

"An ethic without built-in value judgments?" Mike challenged.

"Yes," George answered, "unless you think that the desire to improve yourself is not a universally acknowledged good thing."

"I'll grant that assumption for now, George. But universally acknowledged good things are hard to use in everyday conversation."

"Not true, my lad," George said loudly. "Let me tell you about John Summers. He and I wrote one of America's great unpublished books together, and I learned a lot about teaching from him. He spent some time in New Jersey teaching universal good things."

"New Jersey?" Mike asked skeptically.

"The right part of New Jersey," George said with reverence. "Lots of 200-year-old houses, and a famous university, plenty of money coming in from people who commute to the city. Anyway, he taught high school there. As far as I'm concerned, high school teaching is the front line in our society."

"That's not something I've done," Mike responded. "Tell me what it was like for him."

The Encounter

John had accepted an offer to teach high school in a wealthy New Jersey community just after he finished college. He was delighted to have found a "good job" in a good school. While many of his former classmates took jobs as substitutes in the inner city of New York, he had a position to be envied—a full-time teacher in the Department of Communication Arts, far from the violence and decay of urban education.

During his orientation week, he had met with David Lyman, the principal. Lyman seemed perfectly cast for his job, and he reminded John of an English boarding school master.

"I want to explain your assignments, Mr. Summers." Lyman began. "You'll note that your schedule lists five classes, apart from cafeteria and study hall duty. Two of those classes are 10th-grade public speaking and two are 11th-grade composition. You'll find some recommended texts for both courses in your department library.

"Your other class—which, I believe, begins your day— is Basic Communication Skills for 'Generals', students in the General Education Program. You see, most of our students are highly-motivated young people. Their parents are well-educated—either faculty members at the college or professionals who commute into New York City.

"But," he went on, "we're surrounded by several 'sending districts' of working-class communities that feed into this school system. The students are members of one 'underclass' or another. A few of them will learn enough to escape their situation, but most have neither the ability nor the desire to succeed.

"If you stay with us long enough, you'll be able to teach our better students. Eventually, you may even get to teach the Advanced Placement students, the college-bound kids who are really worth teaching. But I want to prepare you for this year. The 'Generals' are slow, tough and unresponsive. You won't teach them much, but I'll be happy if you can just keep them in line. That won't be easy, I know. But don't become disappointed in yourself if you have difficulties with them."

John recalled those words the next week as he drove slowly through the parking lot filled with teenagers awaiting the start of the school year. "I won't just be a babysitter for these 'Generals'," he thought to himself. "I know I can teach them something that will make a difference in their lives."

As he entered the stately brick building on the way to his first class, he discovered, with relief, that he was not late. The large clock that marked official time and controlled the bells was ten minutes slower that his watch. He had time to stop in his department office.

The office was crowded with students seeking to change their schedules, even though the first class had yet to begin. He was surprised by the contrast between the dignified surroundings and the chaos of the room. At least 15 students from various racial and ethnic origins competed among themselves, each using a different technique for getting the secretary's attention.

John walked into the department library and picked up a carton containing the 25 copies of God is My Co-pilot that he had ordered for his first class. He had hoped that the novel would be simple enough for his 'Generals' yet tough enough to hold their attention. Other teachers had assured him that the story had succeeded in previous classes.

He walked into Room 412 with briefcase and books. He had not been able to examine it before because a renovation project had not been completed until a few days earlier. The classroom was beautiful. Its 12-foot ceilings gave a sense of expansiveness, and its large windows overlooked the nearby university campus. The floor had been newly carpeted, and the student desks had been sanded and stained.

His own desk made a special impact on him. It was made of a dark hardwood that had detailed carving around the drawers, and it was newly stained and waxed. The swivel chair behind the desk was cushioned and looked inviting. "No budget problems here," John thought to himself.

He quickly surveyed his first class. Twenty-five students were talking, laughing, or lounging casually. The noise in the room subsided as he thumped the books on the desk and dropped his briefcase to the floor. He closed the door as the bell rang and officially started his first class.

After introducing himself, he began to call the roll. The artificial quiet of those first few moments faded gradually as he stumbled over the names from unfamiliar languages.

"Can't that dude get my name straight?"

"Who is this guy anyway?"

"Must be new, man. That's for sure!"

Except for an occasional "Here, boss," or "That's me, brother," the class members spoke only to each other, not to him. Despite the catcalls and raucous laughter, he managed to get through the roster of names. Then, picking up his copy of God is My Co-pilot, he slammed it down on the desk and demanded their attention.

His booming voice and the explosive sound of the book brought immediate silence. As he began to pass out the books, he told them that since he was new to them and to the school, they would spend a few minutes getting acquainted. He added, "We'll read this novel during the next two weeks and we'll talk together about the danger and excitement of men at war." He assured them that he would be happy to give them additional help if they had trouble doing the reading; all he asked of them were their best efforts.

After he had passed out the books and sat down behind his large desk, absolute silence filled the room. No one said a word. "Now," he thought to himself, "this is the way it ought to be. They must be waiting for me to begin." He luxuriated in his role, feeling that he was now a teacher. He would impart the wealth of wisdom he had gained in his studies.

As he was about to speak, a massive black student suddenly stood up, shoving his desk roughly aside. Holding the book in his hands he said defiantly, "I ain't gonna read this shit." With one motion he ripped the book in half.

The boy sitting next to him looked up in surprise, then smiled. His skin was very white—as if he had never spent any time outdoors—and his thin, sandy hair stuck out in the back where he had removed his baseball cap. His smile turned to a mocking, uneven grin as he stood and began, with considerable exertion, to tear his book apart.

Dumbfounded, John sat forward in his chair. Before he could think of what to say, all the students in the room—including the girls—followed the lead of the two boys, ripping their books into pieces. Then they sat looking at him, awaiting his response.

John sat behind his imposing desk in his padded chair while panic overtook him. Nothing he had seen or heard in college had prepared him for this. He knew that almost any step he took would be dangerous—perhaps disastrous—but he could not simply sit there.

Various possibilities occurred to him, each one unworkable. If he sent all 25 to the principal's office, he might lose his job and he would certainly be ridiculed by the other faculty members. But some form of discipline seemed to be called for.

He briefly entertained the idea of a show of strength to intimidate them, then rejected the idea. Although he was strong—he had been on his college wrestling team, and he continued to arm wrestle regularly—the hope of bluffing 25 tough kids seemed too tenuous. Visions of different newspaper headlines flashed through his mind: "First Year Teacher Brutalizes Students," or, even worse, "Teacher Beaten in Front of Class." He sat rooted behind his desk, gaping at the ruins of God is My Co-pilot. The title seemed peculiarly ironic.

In order to gain time, he moved slowly around his desk and sat on one corner. Suddenly, he pointed at the boy who had begun the destruction of the books and asked in a steady but angry voice, "Who in the hell do you think you are to take a man's work and rip it in half? Where do you get your authority? Who are you?"

The boy glared back at him, considering the question. After a moment's thought he answered: "I'm the best mechanic you ever met, that's who I am. I can take an engine, tear it down, and put it back together again before you can smoke a cigarette. I'll bet you can't do that, and neither can that guy," he said, gesturing toward the pile of torn books.

The rest of the class members waited, shifting their glance from John to the student. "Too bad he can't figure out a book the way he can an engine," John thought to himself. "But books sure aren't the way to get his attention."

He looked squarely into the student's eyes. "I don't believe you," he said, "but I'll let you prove it. Tell you what. Tomorrow, you run this class. I want you to come in here with two carburetors and show us what you can do. Let's see just how good you are."

"Bet on it, boss," he said, and stood up to leave. John, however, continued speaking to the class. He went on about human dignity and the fruits of labor, trying to make them aware of their wrong in destroying books. As he talked, his words seemed increasingly trivial to him, and he felt he was summarizing the values of Western Civilization in a coach's pep talk. Many of the boys slipped out of the classroom without being challenged by John. When the bell rang at last, he fled to the Faculty Lounge for his only break that day.

In the lounge he tried to salvage his pride and sense of purposefulness in talks with other teachers. They gave him lots of support, and they talked together about the demands of their work, the low pay, and their unappreciative students. Above all, they concluded students do not know what is good for them.

The remaining classes that day were tedious but uneventful. He had the sophomores present short, impromptu talks on the most interesting book they had read over the summer. His junior composition students wrote an in-class essay diagnosing their strengths and weaknesses as writers, and he assigned them to read "Choosing a Topic," the first chapter in their composition text. Despite the enthusiasm his other classes showed, John's thoughts kept returning to his "Generals".

The next morning John felt unusually tense as he drove to work, anticipating his first class. He was torn between roles that seemed to conflict. As a teacher, he felt obligated to impact the collected wisdom of his society and culture, to teach actively. But when he recalled his own years as a student, he sensed that the teachers who had made the most impact on him had not forced knowledge on him. Instead, they had helped him grasp the meaning and general truths of his personal experiences. "And now," he thought with disappointment, "I'm no more than a warden."

He heard no sounds as he approached the classroom door. "I wonder if they're all cutting today?" he asked himself. When he opened the door at the bell, however, he discovered that the room was filled with his students, sitting quietly. The words written on the chalkboard at the front explained the unusual orderliness:

CARBORETION BASICS, 1A
PETER WASHINGTON, INSTRUCTOR
SHUT UP AND LISTEN

"You're late, teach," Pete said from his seat in John's chair. On the desk lay two oily carburetors. John smiled warily and sat in the back of the classroom.

Pete slammed the door shut, seized one of the carburetors, and began talking without further preface. From his seat in the back of the class, John noticed that no one played around. Pete was the biggest and probably the toughest guy in the class, and he used his status to command their attention. More importantly, he knew what he was talking about.

His fingers flew as he tore the carburetor apart, explaining in street idiom what each of the tiny parts was and what it did. Though his vocabulary was that of an eighth-grader, he knew what words to use to describe the device he held. Everyone, even the girls, leaned forward and listened.

When Pete completed his instruction, the class members asked questions, questions that indicated a high degree of understanding of what had been said. As he listened to the discussion, John discovered that, despite his utter ignorance of engines, even he had understood the principles of carburetion.

The bell rang, ending the class, but the discussion continued. John walked to the front and leaned back against the front of the desk. "Who's next?" he asked with a smile. Suddenly, a knot of students formed around him, each demanding his attention.

"I play pool," one voice said.

"I make clothes."

"I collect beer cans."

John found their enthusiasm overwhelming. He felt a tug at his sleeve. "Hey, teach, want to see what I can do?" a male voice said. He turned to see the boy's hand slide from his pocket. John's eye caught the gleam of steel in his hand, and he reacted with instincts honed by years of wrestling matches. Instantly, he seized the boy's wrist and twisted.

As suddenly as it had begun, it was over. The gravity knife lay on the floor while the boy held his wrist tenderly.

"Hey, teach," a voice from the crowd said. "Go easy. Carleton's just high on glue again."

"Maybe so," John responded. "But no one—and I mean no one—pulls a knife around here!" Their wide-open eyes indicated the shock his speed and dexterity had created.

"You," John said, turning to the pale student who had been the second to tear his book apart the day before. "Did you say you play pool?"

"Better'n anybody you ever saw," he drawled. "Want to have class at Leo's?

"No," John said. "I've got a miniature pool table I'll bring in tomorrow. Can you impress us with that?"

"Easy, man," the boy said, walking from the room.

John stooped quickly and picked up the knife, but Carleton was already gone. "I say again: No one pulls a knife around here. Some things aren't all right."

He slipped the knife into his pocket as the rest of the class slowly left the room. He turned to discover Pete collecting the tiny screws and springs from the disassembled carburetor. "All right," John said, "I'm impressed. But this carburetor doesn't look anything like mine. How come?"

"Bet you drive one of them foreign things," Pete said patiently. "They're different."

"How different?" John asked. "How do Italian carburetors differ from American machines?"

"Shit, man, how'm I gonna know that? You think I drive such a car?"

"I didn't know," John replied. "Can you find out about those differences for me?"

"How, man?"

"Try the library."

"The library? Shit, I've never been in the place."

"Give it a try," John said. "That's the only way I know to learn about things I can't do myself."

"Maybe I will. Maybe I won't. I gotta put these things back where I got 'em." Pete stuffed the parts into his coat pocket and left the room.

John sat at his desk, looking at the spots of grease and oil, wondering what steps to take after they became bored with each other's stories. He decided to skip the Faculty Lounge, sensing that none of his colleagues would have the answer to his problem.

The next day he arrived early to set up his miniature pool table. Doug, his resident pool shark, arrived soon carrying what appeared to be a case for a flute. In it lay a pool cue of wood and gold that Doug quickly assembled.

After the class arrived, Doug began his explanation. He talked to them about friction, angles of rebound, and the continental spin. Though hampered by the toy table, it was obvious that Doug knew more about geometry and probability than many high school teachers on the subject.

John would later discover that Doug had failed every math course the school offered, yet he possessed all the innate ability that any teacher could want. As with the preceding day, the class listened and later asked questions.

Even Carleton, who John watched carefully throughout the class, entered into the discussion.

At the end of the class, John established an order for the next five presentations. He then interrupted Doug as he replaced the cue in its case. "You're pretty good," John said.

"The best."

"Oh, yeah? What about Willie Mosconi?"

"Well, that dude's pretty good too, I hear. Never seen him play at Leo's."

"Why don't you find out some more about him and big-time pool players?" John asked.

"Where?"

"Try the library."

The weeks that followed were filled with personal presentations. Every student gave a report or demonstration of what he or she knew best. Subjects ranged from carpentry to baking to sewing. The only constant was that the students listened to one another.

One morning, as John hurried to his class, he was interrupted by the principal, David Lyman. "I've got a proctor in your classroom, Mr. Summers, so they can start without you. Come down to my office, if you would?"

John sensed the ominous note in the invitation, but he knew he couldn't resist. He felt keenly disappointed— today Marty was going to explain how she won every 100-yard dash she ran.

"Sit down, John," Lyman said. "I've had some complaints from Fred Willis, the teacher next to you. He tells me that your first-period class discussions get pretty loud sometimes. And your department tells me that you aren't submitting lesson plans or using the standard texts for that class. I know that I said that I would be happy if you just kept those kids in line. But I think you're doing them a disservice by letting them think they're learning something when all you've got is a B.S. session in there."

"I'm sorry about the noise," John said. "We get pretty carried away sometimes. But," he said forcefully, "those kids are learning something. More than they've learned in past communication classes."

"As I understand it," Lyman responded, "you're just letting them talk about their personal experiences. That isn't education."

"I'd agree with you if I were just letting them talk. But I'm not. Think about it this way. No education does any good unless you can apply it to your own life and experiences. That's why those kids have done so little in school up until now.

"But," he went on, gaining confidence, "personal experiences don't teach them anything without some interpretation and application based on the larger body of knowledge from a teacher. So, you can't learn without application; you can't apply without some learning.

"What everybody forgets about with these kids is the need to apply it so that it fits their lives. The values of this civilization are not self-evident if you come from the part of society that they do. They won't be willing to learn what I know unless they see value in what they already know.

"I assure you that I plan to introduce some readings soon. But for now, they're communicating with each other, they're teaching me some things I didn't know before, and they're getting ready to make the next step—to learn something outside their immediate experience."

"I'm encouraged to hear you say that," Lyman responded. "But remember that we have to maintain standards."

"I think that we can only maintain the standards of the kids who already have them," John said slowly. "But these kids don't know those standards—they haven't been brought up with that same everyday respect for ideas and knowledge.

"And I can't say 'Learn these standards'. That won't help. I have to discover their standards and gain their respect that way. Then we can apply what they know in order to acquire those other standards that you and I think so highly of without demeaning their set of values."

"It sounds good, John, but I think you're naïve. If you're right, I'll nominate you for Distinguished Teacher. If you're wrong, I'm going to urge you to seek professional relocation."

"You're on," John said as he hurried from the office, hoping to hear the rest of Marty's presentation.

He arrived in his classroom just as Marty finished. His students, of course, knew about John's bout with the principal, and they watched his face for clues about the outcome. "Pete," he said confidently, "when do I get my explanation about Italian carbs?"

"Tomorrow, if you want it."

"I want it."

"The next day a new legend appeared on the chalkboard:

ADVANCED CARBURETION
PETER WASHINGTON, INSTRUCTOR
PAY ATTENTION!

John was surprised to see a stack of note cards in Pete's hand, and wondered where he got the idea. Pete talked continuously for the next 40 minutes, illustrating points on the board. He made clear the differences between American and Italian systems, and emphasized his preference for the American approach.

Over the next four weeks each of the students, in turn, presented a follow-up report. While none of the students used the 'King's English', all of them succeeded in making themselves understood.

Discipline problems were rare, usually arising with Carleton. When disruptions did arise, the other students— often led by Pete—would silence then noisy student. "Shut the hell up or get rapped in the mouth" became a favorite saying. Carleton and two other students who were always high on drugs probably learned little, but they did not prevent the others from learning.

When a week remained before the last follow-up report, John appeared in class with a box of books. He walked among the desks, handing each student a copy of Requiem for a Heavyweight. No one tore it up.

"I'd like you to read this before next Wednesday," John said to them. "I picked this story because I think you'll like it. If you don't like it, you can give a report on why you didn't." They nodded their heads, almost in unison.

"By the way," John added. "Anybody here know how to organize a car-washing party?"

"We did one at my church once," Pete said. "How come you want to know?"

"Well, I thought we might like to earn some money so we could have a party before the Christmas break," John said. "Besides, we owe the school $56 for some copies of God is My Co-pilot that got lost."

He watched them smile, then went back to listen to Marty's discussion of training techniques.

The Lesson

"Well," Mike said, "did he keep his job?

"He was named Distinguished Teacher," George responded, "but he left high-school teaching so he could go to graduate school."

"What about the class? Does he ever hear from any of them?"

"He gets a lot of information, but some of it is rather indirect," George answered. "John gets back there for research projects at the university, and he says he's always bumping into one of them. A couple of them operate gas stations, and three or four have become very successful merchants.

"Maybe Pete is the biggest success story. He started acquiring library cards from all over, and carrying a pocket dictionary around. He needed a couple years to get his diploma, but he stuck to it. He eventually wound up going to a small college in the Midwest. Pete apparently improved his grades enough that football recruiters could get him in. Word has it that he loves it out there, but his friends are sure he'll come back to New Jersey sooner or later."

"Does John feel good about what he did?" Mike asked.

"From everything I can gather," George replied, "John feels that he made some life-long friends. Several have told him that he made a real difference in their lives that he allowed them to be themselves first so that they could grow beyond themselves. I'm sure the words are John's, but the sentiments are probably the kids'."

"Almost as if he saw more good in them than they did themselves? Is that it?" asked Mike.

"It's something like that, though John insists that he didn't know what he was going to do until he did it. So, some of it seems to be good instincts.

"But since I brought up this story in talking about judo, it also reminds me of Dr. Kano's Second Maxim, Jitta kyoe, dealing with perfection of others. Dr. Kano stressed that the pursuit of individual perfection was not enough. While personal perfection is necessary, it's not sufficient to produce a better society.

"The problem of focusing only on the individual is that it leads to self-centeredness and that produces conflicts with others. Dr. Kano believed that jitta kyoe—the perfection of the individual—was counter-balanced by jiko no kansei because it emphasizes the welfare and benefit of others."

"In effect, people should strive for perfection in others even as they pursue it for themselves. Is that it?" Mike asked.

"Absolutely. Dr. Kano's two principles reflect a spirit of 'give-and-take', a spirit that improves mutual cooperation and tends to make the whole greater than the sum of the parts."

"That seems to resolve my objection, since there isn't a fixed idea of social good hidden away in the maxim." Mike was silent for a moment. "Can we say that John's success with that 'General' class came from his belief in their ability to become more than they were?"

"Partly, yes," George answered, "but I think it goes even deeper than that. He avoided the errors many teachers make. Despite the pressure from his principal, John saw that he would have to raise their standards by actually listening to them and responding to them, rather than by insisting on his own—or the school's—abstract concept of 'standards'."

"I've watched my two kids go through the high schools," Mike remarked, "and I've spent my share of time in administrative hassles. From that perspective, John acted very bravely given the school and the principles warning."

"I'm pretty sure Dr. Kano would agree with you," George responded. "It did take courage to fight the system. But as I see it, the bravest thing he did was to maintain control over himself, which is also the key to success in judo.

"Remember the book they tore up? However irritated John was by the sacrilege of destroying books, he was probably more upset by the insult to his taste and judgment. He'd tried to make a good choice about the book he wanted them to read, and he liked it himself. So he could easily have found some kind of personal insult when they didn't like it.

"I have to assume that they'd hurt his feelings. But since he was a teacher and had power over them, he didn't need to admit that they'd made him feel bad. He could have used disciplinary processes to get even with them. But he didn't. He stayed in control.

"And there were other points where he could have exploded—think how he must have felt seeing those greasy carburetors on his beloved desk, or how irritated he was when they called him 'teach'.

"But he kept his focus on changing their behavior, not on his own feelings. When he was confronted by resistance, he didn't assume he had the right answer— he didn't try to jam education down their throats. And he didn't just go on talking to himself while they ignored him.

"He saw what every high school teacher needs to see: Resistance does not mean personal rejection. It says 'talk to us, not to the notes you took in college!' I think that's the key aspect of Verbal Judo– knowing the other and accepting their individuality even when it seems a denial of our preferences.

"John maintained a larger view—the view that says society can only get better if you pursue your own goals with a greater good in mind. John was sure enough of himself to consider the kids in that class personally, and in that way he helped them raise their own expectations of what they could be."

"The 'larger good' that keeps coming up, then, must be self-improvement. Right?" Mike asked.

"That's certainly the way I see it," George responded. "American society is built, from day one, on the notion that anyone or any group can improve, if only they have initiative. Anything that increases another person's initiative has to be a 'larger good'."

"Then how do we put that as a principle of Verbal Judo?" Mike asked. "John's success came from motivating his students to improve themselves, and he did this by raising their expectations of what they could be. Is that our principle?"

That's our principle, all right," George responded. "But I think it can be put more simply."

Motivate others by raising their expectations of themselves.

"There might be such a thing as Verbal Judo after all," Mike said appreciatively. "Let's take a break up here in

4

The Language of Persuasion

The Challenge

Williams. Then I'll do the driving for a while."

"Anyone who orders chicken-fried steak for lunch has no grounds to complain about my breakfasts," George laughed as their waitress walked away after taking their order.

"It's a habit I picked up while I was working regularly in Texas," Mike answered defensively. "Besides, it's their house specialty." He paused for a moment. "Did you ever notice how much people talk about food on long drives?"

"Let's talk about Verbal Judo instead," George said enthusiastically. "Think how many individuals who have to work with people need defined strategies to get things done in a predictable manner."

"Let's not get ahead of ourselves here," Mike answered. "I'm optimistic too, but I think we still have a lot to work out. We still only have a name—a good name, I concede—that may not suggest to people what we're talking about. We still need to find out what people think when they hear the phrase, Verbal Judo."

"What line of work are you two gentlemen in?" The deep male voice next to them forced their heads to turn simultaneously. Above the partition separating their table from the next they saw a large, florid face topped by a mass of flowing gray hair.

"I heard you mention Verbal Judo," the smiling face said. "That sounds like something I could use to twist the arms of my customers and make some sales." His last three words reverberated through the diner.

George winced at the salesman's suggestion and demurred. "Probably not," he answered. "Judo is primarily a defensive tactic."

"And I'll bet you think that selling is offensive," the man said wryly, obviously pleased with his play on words. With that, he stood and faced them across the divider. He was wearing a bright yellow shirt, cut in a western style. Around his neck was a string tie, held at the collar by a large piece of turquoise-encrusted silver. "You boys should give an old salesman a break," he said, counting out change for a tip.

"What are you selling?" George asked with interest. Mike's eyes rolled upward. He had seen George plunge into hour-long conversations with strangers before, and he did not want to lose driving time.

"Insurance. I'll bet you gentlemen don't need any," he said jovially.

"That's so," George responded. "But I'll buy you a

piece of pie if you can persuade me that selling isn't an aggressive activity."

"Persuading is what I do best," the man said, collecting his coat and circling the partition to join them. "No dessert, though," he continued, embracing his considerable girth with both hands. "But I will have more coffee."

The Encounter

"You two dress like desperados," the salesman said, indicating their leather jackets and denim pants. "But I can tell from your haircut and hands that you have some kind of desk jobs. What do you do?"

"We're consultants," George said simply.

"Consultants?" the man asked with mock gravity. "Doesn't a consultant borrow your watch to tell you what the time is, then send you a bill? Is that what you two do?"

Mike shifted uneasily in the booth, then brightened. "Maybe," he said. "Depends on how you look at it. George here teaches people in business and government to speak more effectively. I do the same thing with writing. Our clients can already talk and write when we arrive, so it's a little like borrowing their watch. But they can do it better when we leave, so we give them something for their money."

"Your friend is very serious," the man remarked to George while chuckling. "He must think Willy Loman joined him for lunch."

Mike turned to the man beside him. "Since you know Death of a Salesman, maybe you can tell us why salesmen have such an image problem."

"Exactly," George agreed. "You were going to tell me that selling isn't an aggressive activity. I'm listening."

The older man turned again to Mike. "You say you teach writing. Does that mean spelling and punctuation—that sort of thing?"

"No," he answered. "The people I work with are pretty good at that. But they need 'design' help. They have to get their point across even if their readers aren't especially interested in the topic."

"That's what I thought," the salesman responded. "I do the same thing."

"How's that?" asked George earnestly? "I thought you said you were a salesman."

"I am, but I'm also explaining why my way of selling isn't offensive," he replied. "Look at it this way. Most people who write use up a lot of effort trying to say exactly what's on their mind, but that's all wasted energy if no one makes the effort to read it. Smart writers figure out first what their reader wants and needs to know and they write that."

"You should teach my classes," Mike said. "I usually spend two days trying to make that point. How did you figure all that out?"

"Don't you think people write reports in the insurance business?" the man asked. "My name's Phil Garber. I've been doing this line of work for 53 years."

"Is that right?" Mike asked.

"Not right, but it's so," Phil responded. "I've got a couple years on Ronald Reagan. I sold insurance back before the Depression, and right through those hard times, and then during the war. For twenty years I ran the national sales office for a company in Dallas. They retired me five years ago—when I turned 73. I've got a place south of here near the Colorado River—right across from California—where I can watch the sun set on London Bridge.

"But I get bored after a few weeks of sitting, so I get out my car and briefcase and start making calls. I love to get out and meet people. Let me tell you both, selling is a wonderful line of work."

"I don't think I've ever heard anyone say that before," Mike marveled.

"You should have," Phil laughed. "You probably went to college too long. You don't learn the downright enjoyment of pressing the flesh with an old fashioned handshake in school.

"But," he went on, "I don't want to pick on you. Lots of people are down on salesmen, not just you."

"I'm not down on anybody," Mike said defensively as George leaned back in the booth, grinning. "I think that George and I both sense something exploitive about selling as a profession. If we're wrong, we want to know. We'll listen to you."

"Boys," the old man said gleefully, "that's the best offer I've had in years."

"You were talking about the way good writers use their readers' lack of interest to get their point across," George said.

"Right," Phil responded. "Well, a salesman can do the same thing. He can use all his energy trying to break down people's resistance and make them buy something or he can use their resistance to persuade them. Isn't that what judo does, use the other person's energy?" Their conversation paused while the waitress brought their orders.

"Sure," said George. "But I thought you wanted to 'twist some arms'?"

"A figure of speech," he said with a wave. "Besides, when I close a sale I do want all the leverage I can get. But the reason I asked about your Verbal Judo idea was to get some new ways to break through the resistance most people have these days to being sold something."

"Why do you say 'these days'? Haven't people always resisted being sold?" George asked.

"Not at all. Selling has been the most important social activity for centuries. It's only recently developed a bad reputation. My wife and I like to take our motor home and head down to Mexico. In the small towns, market day is a real social event, and the people who have interesting things to sell are local heroes.

"And that isn't true only in foreign countries. Think of the importance people put on salesmen back during the frontier period here in this country. The most important event in a six-month span was the arrival of a peddler with things to sell, new items to tempt people who longed for a chance to buy something new."

"Was it advertising that changed all that?" Mike asked. "Those social events you described work because people go to buy things they want or need. But ads try to force people to buy things beyond their needs and means."

"You've got a point," the older man responded. "But I don't think advertising is the villain here. People have always wanted to be successful, to provide some hard evidence of their success, and to add to the enjoyment of living. You really can't persuade a person to want something that displeases them. You're both old enough to remember the Edsel automobile, aren't you?

"I guess you could say that," Mike answered, surprised at his own vanity. Why did he hesitate to reveal his age to a man 35 years his senior?

"Now," Phil went on, "lots of people confuse salesmen with con men -- I guess because confidence men often pretend to be salesmen. But even a con man can only persuade people who already want something for nothing, whether it's found money or a miracle stock."

"All right," George said, pushing back his plate. "I'll accept that there are more social values in sales than I thought. That still leaves the question of whether selling is aggressive."

"Bad salesmen might be aggressive, but good ones never are," Phil said. "If I say, 'Want to buy some insurance?' to a prospect, 99 times out of 100 he'll say 'no', because everybody naturally resists aggressiveness. Once they resist, I'll have to waste a lot of energy trying to make them buy.

"And it's the same way in a store. When the clerk says, 'May I help you?' people feel that's aggressive—who knows why? So they resist what sounds like aggression and say, 'No, just looking', even when they really do need some advice.

"A good salesman—like me—will never make that kind of direct statement and challenge the customer's ability to resist. Instead, I talk with people and listen to what they have to say. If I was a clerk in a store, I'd watch what people were looking at and I'd say 'We have more of those over here', or something to show that my interest in them went beyond taking their money. In my line of work, I listen for certain clues that indicate their needs, especially the needs that they don't even know about.

"Sooner or later, I'll ask them if they feel fully protected. People make jokes about insurance salesmen, but nobody who's ever had a catastrophe happen ever complained about having too much insurance. The people who never need it—they laugh and tease us. So what?

"Some people have all the coverage they need—they feel fully protected. Some people do, and that's that. But most people will at least consider the question, and that's where persuasion starts.

"You see, selling is filled with unknowns. But there is one thing I can always count on with every prospect.

Someplace, in the back of their head, there's a voice that says 'I won't be sold'. If I contradict that voice, I won't make a sale. Instead, I agree with that voice and say 'Of course you don't want to be sold. I'm here to help you make a reasonable decision'."

"That's interesting," Mike said. "A friend of mine who's an amateur magician explained a technique to me called equivoque. It's based on the premise that every subject a magician works with has an inner voice that says 'I won't be tricked'. So you trick them by using that attitude. Equivoque, according to my friend, means that you tell the subject 'Do whatever you want to do' and then you watch while he does just what you want him to do."

"Now I've learned something," Phil said with a laugh. "I like that idea. Like I said, selling and buying are social activities. People are entertained by the experience, whether they admit it or not. People who go to magic shows insist that they don't want to be tricked, but why are they there, then? The same is true of my prospects. They act like they don't want to buy, but they could always throw me out.

"Equivoque, huh? I like that word. Write the word down on one of your business cards for me so I can find it in the dictionary."

"Of course you don't want that card so you can send me some literature later, right?" Mike asked.

"You're learning," the older man chuckled. "Persuading, as I see it, takes a series of steps. Each step is a resistance point, a voice that says 'don't buy'. I listen to each step and

I agree with the prospect. Once I've agreed, they'll usually listen to my explanation, and we can go up the next step. Once we get to the top of the steps, his enthusiasm's bound to be at its highest. So I suggest that it's time to act. Most times he agrees with me."

"I think I follow what you're saying," George added. "But even if I accept the general idea that people enjoy the experience of buying, it doesn't mean that we need salesmen."

"That's a nice-looking ring," Phil said, pointing to the turquoise jewelry George wore. "Did you buy that on the reservation?"

"No, at a shop. I wouldn't know how to tell good jewelry from bad if I went out on my own."

"There's your answer," Phil said. "You wanted someone to remove some risk for you. That's what salesmen do. When some actor endorses a product, most people know that he probably doesn't like that brand better than another. But they can be sure that this person—who is deeply concerned about his reputation—wouldn't attach his name to something that would embarrass him.

"And that's what the salesman does. He puts his credibility on the product and gives it a personal sense of worth. 'Buy it because someone like me is selling it', he says.

"The point you made about advertising earlier is only partly true. I read somewhere that scientists find solutions to problems before we even know what the problems are. Well, that's true of products and services. How can anybody keep informed about all the things that would satisfy them or make them happy? Just think how busy people are.

"So salesmen act like old-fashioned town criers. They go around yelling out the news, telling everybody about their product. Now, not everybody is interested—did you know that the folks who send out mailers think that they're doing real well if just 2% of the people answer? And so a lot of uninterested people have to hear news intended for a small number of interested people—people who don't even know they should be interested.

"That's inefficient and frustrating for the salesman and for the people who won't become customers. But if you have a better way to go about it, let me know. If not, I'll just keep being inefficient and talking to lots of folks."

"Your love for your work seems rare," Mike said.

"I don't think so," Phil responded. "People who sell find the work very exciting. Making a sale is a dramatic event, filled with tension and real consequence. It's like an Olympic competition every day. What you're trying to do is to get them to act, to use their own resistance to sell themselves."

George took the check from the table and stood up. "Give me one of your cards. I want to keep in touch." They exchanged the pieces of cardboard as they walked to the cashier.

"Where did you say you were going?" Phil asked Mike as they waited for George to pay the bill.

"Las Vegas," Mike answered. "Going on business, though."

"A long drive. You have a company car or your own?"

"Mine," Mike said. "Why do you ask?

"Just curious. You probably checked to be sure your insurance would cover you while using the car for business. I mean, you'd hate to have something happen and not be protected."

Mike's face expressed his concern. "I don't understand why I wouldn't be covered," he said.

"Let me explain," Phil said, walking outside with him.

The Lesson

Mike drove for several hours after leaving Williams. To counter their growing restlessness, they tested the upper volume levels of the car's tape player. When the thunderous music stopped at the end of a tape, Mike turned off the machine. "George, did I get taken?" he asked, indicating the contract on the dashboard. "Do you think I really need trip insurance?"

"Well, whatever the case we got our money's worth," George said laughing. "I have a whole new attitude about selling and salespeople, and I see how a sale relates to Verbal Judo."

"Tell me," Mike responded. "If Phil is right about the

social importance of selling, then we have to concede that most attempts to persuade people are a kind of selling."

"That's how I figure it" George said. "It's so basic, in fact, that it reminds me of ogoshi."

"What's that?

"Ogoshi is a basic hip throw, the most basic move in judo. It's the one all beginners learn before attempting more complicated throws. Beginners start on it because it illustrates Dr. Kano's Third Maxim of Judo, Seiryoku zenryo.

"Seiryoku zenryo is a simple maxim, but a powerful one. It says that you must achieve maximum efficiency with minimum effort in everything that you do."

"Isn't that the principle behind all judo moves?" Mike asked.

"Sure," George answered. "But the point is harder to see in the more advanced moves, because they assume that your opponent is already coming at you aggressively. You react to their action.

"Ogoshi is not just a reactive technique. Like all persuasion, you begin with the need to move someone from one position to another. It doesn't make any difference if the position is a physical one or a state of mind.

"You've probably seen ogoshi in some of the demonstrations I've put on. At the start, we seem only to be grappling—hanging on to each other's upper body. But as soon as my opponent starts to move, I anticipate the direction, step in front of him, and twist my body sideways in the same direction. My movement puts my hip in front of him. Since we're both going in the same direction, our combined momentum throws him up and over my hip. When I time the throw exactly and keep my balance, it feels almost as if the opponent has come willingly."

"I'm sure I've seen that," Mike said. "But tell me how that move relates to persuading."

"If you try to throw someone over your hip that is resisting you, the result is a pointless tugging and pulling and the stronger opponent would counter and overcome you. Remember that ogoshi only works if you're moving with the other person. You have to time your throw to synchronize with your opponent's movements.

"In selling, you want to 'make your move' on a customer, but if you try to force it you'll run into the natural tendency to resist. People sit back on their heels and counter your efforts. And since they can always say 'no,' they can always win.

"But remember that Phil talked about paying attention and listening to the customer, trying to learn what they needed and wanted, even if they couldn't identify it. That's a lot like judo, because it's the balance gives you leverage and direction."

"Phil did talk about selling as if it were an athletic competition," Mike added. "I wonder if a good sale feels to him like a successful ogoshi feels to you?

"I'm sure of that," George said," or he wouldn't have been so enthusiastic about his work. He gets real satisfaction from it. And just as my opponents come onto the mats voluntarily, Phil figures that people do want to be sold."

"Is there a way to say that as a maxim for Verbal Judo?" Mike asked.

"Sure. It isn't too different from Dr. Kano's principle.

Persuade others with their energy, not your own.

"I like that," Mike said. "It makes me feel positively about a skill that I've always been suspicious of."

As they spoke, the windshield appeared to burst into flame. "This is the curse that afflicts all who drive west across this desert," Mike said, trying to find the road through the glare of the setting sun. "November days do end early."

"How long 'til we get to Vegas?" George asked.

"Just over two hours. But I'd rather stop in Kingman and stretch while the sun goes down. Then you can drive to Vegas."

"I'd rather push ahead," George responded. "I don't think I can do another road town."

"Don't forget that we pick up an hour—there's a time change in Nevada," Mike insisted. "Besides, this place is different. The main road through town is named in honor of Andy Devine."

"Now that's worth a stop."

5

The Language of Supervision

The Challenge

They left the lights of Kingman to discover that full darkness had fallen on the desert. After driving more than 500 miles on the interstate in sunlight, they now found themselves on a two-lane road.

The narrow road twisted across the uneven desert floor, and oncoming traffic focused their combined attention on the road. In open stretches, however, when they faced no opposing lights, the dark engulfed them. No lights were visible within the limits of their vision.

"How do they find people to work out here?" George asked, gesturing toward the wilderness surrounding them. "It seems hard to believe that we'll suddenly come to a city of half-a-million people here in the middle of nowhere."

"I guess the frontier has always drawn people looking for another chance," Mike said. "In terms of job opportunity, Las Vegas is the best shot lots of people have. Most of the jobs in the resort business don't require a lot of highly specialized skills, just the willingness to do service work.

"That must be the place," George said, indicating an aurora of light ahead of them.

"Has to be," Mike agreed. "I'm anxious to be there. The chance to work out problems with Verbal Judo has been exciting, but I'm worn out. What I want now is a hassle-free evening. Get checked in, get some dinner, and get some rest."

"I'll go along with that," George added, "But I plan to spend some time at the blackjack tables before I get any sleep."

The desert ended suddenly, and the brilliant lights of the Strip made driving difficult. "Help me locate our hotel," Mike asked.

"That's not hard." George said, pointing through the windshield at a sign more than 10 stories high. Their client had arranged for accommodations at one of the Strip's best-known casinos, and a spectacular display of colored lights announced it to anyone within miles.

The Encounter

Mike pulled into the registration area. A bellman, whose uniform recalled old Phillip Morris cigarette advertisements, approached their car. "Welcome to Las Vegas," he said in tones of genuine friendliness. "Are you gentlemen checking in?"

Mike assured him that they were. The young man

unloaded their suitcases quickly and stacked them on a hand truck as Mike surrendered the car to be parked. "Follow me, gentlemen," the bellman said. "I'll get you registered."

He led them through a series of automatic doors into a brightly-lit lobby. They crossed the marble floors to the end of a line of people that snaked through a labyrinth of velvet ropes. "There will be only a short wait before you check in, gentlemen," the bellman said. "I'll be close by with your bags and I'll take them to your room for you as soon as you're ready."

Mike thanked him while he surveyed the line. At least 50 people were ahead of them, although it was impossible to estimate how many different parties were waiting. At the front of the line, people remained in place until a registration clerk was available.

The check-in area, Mike thought, seemed to combine a race track's betting windows and a bank's cashier cages. The counters were made of gray marble, and a grating covered each opening. Only three of the twelve windows were occupied.

The clerks who worked behind the cages looked as if they had just left a wedding. Each wore a slate-gray morning coat. Their white shirts were pleated and studded; precise bow ties were knotted at their throats. On their hands were tight gloves that matched their coats.

Mike and George had stood in line for several minutes without making significant progress toward their goal when the bellman returned. "Excuse me," he said to Mike, "are you a professor at Berkeley?"

"I was, until a few years ago," Mike responded. "Why do you ask?"

"I audited a course you taught," he answered. "You probably don't remember me—David Fischer."

"Of course," Mike said enthusiastically. "You were working on a doctorate in medieval aesthetics."

"Correction, I'm still working on it," David said with an ironic chuckle. "This job lets me work at night so I can have days free to write my dissertation. Listen, I have to go check my station, but I'll be back in a few minutes."

Mike and George spent the next few minutes reviewing encounters they had had with former students. Then George followed the line with his eyes and looked toward the ceiling. "They've only got three check-in windows open. This could take forever. I'll be back in a minute," he added. "I just want to take a look at the casino."

Twenty minutes later he re-entered the lobby, to discover Mike standing at the head of the line talking to the bellman named David. "What's the hold up here?" George asked, hoping to distract the conversation from his prolonged absence.

"The hotel just installed new billing software in the computers," David answered. "The check-in clerks are having a lot of trouble with it."

"I thought they were trying to discourage business," Mike said. "At least we should be next." His words became fact almost immediately as a group left the second of the three open windows and headed for the elevator. David excused himself as Mike and George stepped to the window.

"Good evening," George said to the clerk, who nodded in acknowledgement. Mike gave their names and that of their client while the clerk tapped the information into a computer terminal with his gloved fingers.

"I'll need your driver's licenses, and a major credit card from each of you as guarantee of payment," he said briskly."

"I don't make the policies, sir," the clerk said without an expression. "You will not be permitted to check in unless you can provide positive identification."

Mike interrupted George's response before he spoke. "We don't want to question policy," he said as he took out his wallet. George reluctantly did the same.

As soon as he acquired the desired articles, the clerk disappeared into the back. George and Mike stood uncomfortably at the check-in window as the minute passed. "Hassle-free evening indeed," George grumbled. "Why can't these people make a simple process like this happen quickly?" He left his place at the window and paced across the lobby, finally taking up a spot at the entrance to the casino, his arms crossed firmly across his chest.

"I'll need your driver's license and a major credit card as a guarantee of payment." Mike turned back to the window at the words, but no one was there. He glanced around and discovered that the request came from the clerk at the window to his right.

Mike looked at the object of the clerk's address to discover a young couple standing nervously at the next window. The man was about 19 and his face looked as if he had worked outdoors most of his life. He was wearing a dress-green Army uniform, and he held his cap under his left arm. "Probably just out of basic training," Mike thought, noting the absence of insignia on his sleeves and his closely cropped hair.

The woman beside him wore a short white party dress and a small white hat with a veil pinned to it. In her left hand—the hand that bore a small but glittering diamond ring—she clasped a large envelope embossed with pink letters:

PHOTOGRAPHIC MEMORIES FROM THE LITTLE CHAPEL OF THE PINES. DO NOT BEND.

The couple appeared confused as they looked first at each other, then at the clerk. The soldier removed his wallet, unfolded it, and held it in front of the clerk's face. He spoke slowly, in a nasal drawl. "This here's my military I.D.," the young man said firmly. Then he added softly, "I don't have no credit card."

"I can't check you in without positive identification," the clerk said. "If you don't have a credit card, I'll have to ask you for full payment in cash, in advance."

"I already sent you a check," the soldier said angrily, his face turning red. "I'm not going to pay you twice."

Mike noticed that David was standing near the registration desk, watching the exchange. The clerk tapped his computer's keyboard, paused then studied his monitor. "The computer doesn't show any record of that payment, sir. If you're not prepared to pay for the room sir, you'll have to step aside."

"Don't you sir me, fella," the soldier responded in a hoarse whisper. "Look here. "We've been planning this day for four months, ever since I went in the service. We just got married this afternoon, right down the street. But then we had to stand in line here for half an hour, and now you tell me you lost the money I sent—I sent a cashier's check from Ft. Riley, just like the lady told me to on the phone when I called two months ago -- and now you say we can't have our room."

"You'll have to talk to my supervisor, sir," the clerk said. "I can't do anything to help you."

"The hell you can't help me," the soldier said through clenched teeth. "You just stand there and look in your com-pu-ter some more until you find my money and get us in our room."

"Don, please," the young woman said, her voice breaking, "let's not spoil our wedding day. I'm sure it's just a mistake."

"I'm not going to let them push us around like this, Patti," he said, embracing her awkwardly. He turned again to the clerk and pointed his finger at him. "Did you hear me?" he raged. "You better find my reservation and my money."

The guests waiting to register were too far from the argument to overhear the conversation, but they sensed that something was wrong. Mike had been in Las Vegas often enough to anticipate the outcome of this exchange, and he looked around the lobby for signs of the hotel's security force. Instead, he caught sight of a large man hurrying toward the desk. In his hotel tuxedo he looked like the father of the bride. His coat was like those worn by the registration clerks, except it had elaborate embroidery that distinguished it. He walked quickly to the window.

"What's the matter here, Henson?" he asked sharply.

The clerk continued to gaze at his monitor for several seconds. Then he looked at the older man from the corner of his eye. "No problem, Mr. Sorenson. This party has no credit card. Policy says I can't check them in without a full cash prepay, which they apparently don't have," he answered.

"That's not it at all," the soldier interrupted, showing the supervisor a fistful of bills. "I sent in payment for three nights in your place—for our honeymoon. And he says he can't find any record of it."

"Let me take a look," the large man said as he circled the registration area. He walked to the computer terminal and worked its keys. "Henson," he said loudly, "look at this." The clerk slowly turned his head toward the screen. "Don't you know how to read these codes yet?" his supervisor demanded. "You have to use a separate access code to find out prepay information. How many times do I have to tell you? Go ahead and take your break now. I'll finish this."

The supervisor stepped to the window and spoke cordially with the young couple, calming the soldier's anger. The clerk named Henson stared coldly at his supervisor's back for a few minutes, then walked into the office.

George was suddenly at Mike's side. "Now what's going on?" he asked.

"Man meets computer," Mike answered quietly. "David is apparently right about the source of the delay."

"Gentlemen, thank you for your patience." Mike and George turned back to the counter. Their clerk handed them their licenses and cards. "Will you be paying for these rooms with cash of your credit cards?"

"We're not paying," George put in. "These rooms are supposed to be prepaid."

Mike felt an overwhelming sense of déjà vu as the clerk stared into his computer monitor. "That isn't what my records say. I have to have full payment in advance."

"I don't care what your records say," George said angrily. "Our rooms were paid in advance by the party making the reservation. Call them and get this straight."

"There are pay phones across the lobby," the clerk said. "I don't think you'll find anybody working this time of night."

"We can solve the problem in the morning," Mike said, hoping to save the rest of the evening. "We'll give you the cost of the rooms now. Then, when we contact our client in the morning and we get this accounting squared away, you can reimburse us."

"You'll have to work that out with them yourselves," the clerk said. "We don't make direct refunds in that way."

Mike noticed the supervisor's stare turn toward the clerk in front of them. He chose to avoid creating another scene. "That's okay," he said, putting a card on the counter. "We'll work it out later."

The clerk ran the plastic through his imprinter quickly, then returned it. "Did you have any luggage, sir?"

David was suddenly at the counter. "My shift ended a few minutes ago, so another bellman will help you with your bags. Do you want to meet me in the Keno Bar for a drink later?"

"Great idea," Mike said. "See you there in 30 minutes." Mike handed the new bellman the room keys, glancing at his watch. He and George followed the young man to the elevator, wondering over the lost 90 minutes.

Half an hour later, Mike and George entered the Keno Bar that overlooked the casino floor. They saw David, now dressed in a sports jacket, sitting at a table with a stunning and impeccably groomed woman.

David stood up as they reached the table. "Good evening," he said, then introduced Mike and George. "This is my fiancée, Sandy Krantz. I was just telling her about the crisis at the registration desk."

"I'd think you would have more exciting things to talk about," George remarked, smiling.

"I find it very interesting," Sandy said with a brilliant

smile. "I've been a supervisor for about six months, and I want to learn all I can."

"Do scenes like that one go on a lot around here?" Mike asked.

"A lot more than management would like to admit," David said thoughtfully, "because they're part of the problem. They send a hidden message to the staff that says you can treat small-time spenders that way."

"But that's only a small part of the problem," Sandy said. "The real problem, if you ask me, is poor supervision."

"It seems to me that the hotel's policy is the source of the problem," Mike said. "After all, the crisis that I saw happened because the clerk was following policy."

"The problem isn't the policy," Sandy replied. "All big organizations have to have policies that define what we can do for the customer, and some customers are bound to get irritated by some of the policies."

"If you ask me," George volunteered, "the problem is in their computer."

They do have some glitches in the system," David said, "but they aren't major. I agree with Sandy, supervisors like Sorenson make everything worse."

"Why's that?" Mike asked. "He was just trying to help that couple."

"That's not how I understand it," Sandy responded. "He should have fixed the problem before it happened, not intervene the way he did."

"That's a nice theory," George said. "But you weren't there. That couple was being treated badly. We can't forget their needs. There's no excuse for the way that G.I. was treated."

"Sure," David agreed. "But that's no excuse for the way the clerk was treated either. Sorenson does that at all the time, and all the clerks on his shift are abrupt with his customers. People who feel criticized aren't going to provide good service."

"Actually," Sandy said, "it's probably not even this man Sorenson's fault. I'm sure he didn't get his job because he had the makings of a good supervisor. It was mostly by accident."

"What do you men, 'by accident'?" Mike asked.

"Have you ever heard of the Peter Principle?" Sandy asked.

"Sure," Mike answered. "I can almost quote it: 'In a hierarchy, every employee tends to rise to his or her level of incompetence'. It's usually applied to big corporations."

"I've never heard the 'official' version before," David said, "but I guess that's what I mean. Sandy and I always say that the hotels keep promoting people who are doing good jobs to spots where they fail. Then they stop promoting them."

"You see," Sandy explained, "if you don't know what you're supposed to do as a supervisor, you might assume that being the boss means telling people what to do, taking long lunches, and getting a parking spot with your name on it."

"That's the way lots of bosses see it," George said. "But don't most supervisors get trained before they start?"

"Well," she said, "I work for another hotel just down the Strip. A few months ago I was promoted to run their catering operation, which put me in a supervisory position. I had a few days of classes, but the training only talked about what to do, not how to go about it. The experiences I've had tell me the most important thing you have to figure out as a supervisor is what to call yourself."

"Titles are important to people," Mike said. "But can changing that change the way people act?"

"I'm not talking about the title that the organization gives you," Sandy answered. "I'm talking about how we think about ourselves.

"Maybe I can explain. When I was 12 or 13, I went to lots of baseball games. My father was a devout Chicago Cubs fan—we lived only a few blocks from Wrigley Field. After my older brother went into the service, my father would take me along on summer afternoons when he could get off from work. I loved to watch the games.

"That was the first time I heard the word 'manager' and I didn't like it very much. I had a crush on all the players, especially the pitchers. But there was this older man—the manager—who bossed them around. If one of them threw the ball wrong, this old guy would come trotting out onto the field and gripe at him. I didn't really know what they were saying out there on the mound, but I always imagined the manager was chewing him out. That's why the pitcher always looked at the ground whenever the manager came out—he was embarrassed."

"I still wonder how grown men feel being told what to do while thousands of people are watching," David remarked.

"Maybe they don't feel so bad since they're making so much money," George suggested.

"Maybe," David said, "but the books on supervision Sandy showed me talk about a theory of human needs by a man named Maslow. Do you know about it?"

"Sure," George responded. "Abraham Maslow's Pyramid of Needs. It shows up in lots of management theories."

"Well," David went on, "if I remember it correctly, things like money are fairly low on his pyramid. The higher need is to feel good about ourselves."

"That seems accurate," Mike said. "We do have to worry about the 'higher' needs. But satisfying the needs at the top of the pyramid is the goal of life."

"That's right," David said. "And the key to feeling good about yourself is the need for independence. That desk clerk lost his independence when his supervisor stepped in. I'll bet he doesn't feel very good about himself, even now."

"I agree with David," Sandy said. "People want independence. The only way supervisors can give them that is to prepare their staff before they meet the customer. They can intervene like baseball managers stepping out of the dugout. They have to be more like directors."

"You mean like a member of the board of directors?" George asked. "Or a movie director?"

"More like the director of a play," Sandy answered. "I studied theatre in college, and I've put on lots of plays. Once I earn a stake here, I'm heading for New York to be a director."

David shook his head, grinning. "Sandy tells stories constantly about how sensitive actors are. 'If you hurt their feelings', she says, 'they'll sulk. And they'll find ways to get even with you'."

"The truth is," Sandy said, "nobody wants to be told what to do, and you can't make them do something. I'll rehearse a scene over and over with some of my actors. And when opening night comes, I'll sit out in the audience and watch them change lines or do things totally different.

"After the performance, I'll ask them why they changed it. They always say that 'It seemed like a good idea'. If I say it was a bad idea, they'll give a worse performance the next time. I've learned that good directors expect that sort of independence."

"Actors are difficult people," George observed.

"It isn't just actors," Sandy went on. "I have to supervise 24 people, and I watch lots of other supervisors. The problems seem to be the same as they are for directors: You can't make people do things like respond to customers or act courteously. You have to encourage them, to direct them, so they'll act in the way you want them to on their own."

"Amen," David said. "The good supervisors in this hotel don't 'manage' or 'manipulate' people. They prepare them so that they can act independently. And when they don't do what you want them to do, you assume that you made a mistake when you were directing them."

"But wait," George protested. "Aren't there poor workers and incompetent people? You can't deny a manager's right to criticize poor performance."

"I'm not sure I agree with you," Sandy said. "Every employee deserves an evaluation of how well she or he is doing the job, and sometimes that evaluation has to point out poor performance.

"But evaluations can't take place in public because the employee can't learn in that situation. When we're criticized, most of us react defensively. We'd rather not hear those words. If other people are around, we'll never learn from the critique. We'll be too busy justifying ourselves."

"Sometime," George said to the couple, "we'll have to tell you about Verbal Judo. But right now, I have an appointment to collect some money from the blackjack tables."

The Lesson

Mike and George next met at dinner the following evening. "Are you winning?" Mike asked.

"I'm not so much winning as I am playing with their money," George responded with satisfaction. "But it's strange; since our talk with David and Sandy, I've been more conscious of the quality of the service I get."

"Have you considered Sandy's ideas about directing in relationship to Verbal Judo?" Mike asked.

"Yeah," George answered enthusiastically. "I think it's perfect. We've been saying all along that the goal of Verbal Judo is to use your words strategically, rather than to say what you feel.

"A director wants to achieve a specific effect, but he can't tell the actors 'create this effect'. Instead, he has to choose his words so that other people, different from him, will create that effect when he isn't there.

"And I think that's what supervisors do. They can't tell their employees what results to produce. They have to encourage independent action, actions that will lead to the results they want."

"I'm a bit surprised," Mike said. "You're such a believer in 'situational rhetoric'. I thought that you would have thought of ways to use Verbal Judo to discipline employees."

"I'll go along with Sandy on that point," George answered. "Supervision should take place in private."

"Isn't that difficult when the work is done in public?" Mike asked.

"What happens in public is a symptom of the problem," George said. "The problem has to be dealt with one-on-one. Even you and I could see the symptoms last evening while we were standing in line. It didn't take any great skill in observing. Why wasn't that supervisor noticing those long lines, then trying to see what form of training or encouragement was needed?

"Instead, he got frustrated because things weren't happening the way he wanted them to. And he took his frustration out on that clerk. More than that, he made everybody who works for him that much less willing to do their best."

"Right," Mike responded. "And the result is more work for the supervisor. Watching that guy take charge of those customers last night reminded me of a principle that one of my clients in Washington, D.C. cities. He calls it the 'I Might As Well Do It Myself' rule."

"Explain," George said.

"Think of it this way," Mike answered. "When you do it yourself, you use up your time but you get more predictable results. When you have an employee do it, you save your time but you lose some predictability."

"That's the same kind of unpredictability Sandy described last night when she was talking about directing, true?"

"Exactly," Mike said. "When supervisors don't give their staff a sense of direction and purpose, that lack of predictability becomes critical. So supervisors have to step in and do it themselves.

"See, supervisors have to value their own time, or they won't try to conserve it by providing direction—direction that ensures more predictable results from the employees."

"In some ways, we're back where we started talking," George said.

"How's that?"

"When I first described Verbal Judo to you at the start of this trip, I talked about Dr. Kano's principle of seiryoku zenryo, the goal of achieving maximum effect with minimum effort."

"I remember," Mike said.

"That principle seems to characterize good supervision," George continued. "If supervisors intrude into their employees' performance, they waste their own time and lose the employees' best efforts—a contradiction of siryoku zenryo. In order to achieve seiryoku zenryo, you have to make your efforts at the right time—before the employees encounter situations where they have to act independently and appropriately."

"Do we have a principle here for Verbal Judo?" Mike asked.

"We do indeed," George responded.

Direct others rather than control them.

"Good, and just in time," Mike concluded. "Our waiter approaches with our dinners."

"Terrific," George said. "I feel lucky, and I want to get back to the casino. Let's not talk about Verbal Judo until we start back."

6

The Language of Negotiation

The Challenge

The early morning sun warmed the desert as they started their return, three days after their journey to Las Vegas. They rode together in silence for the first hour, perhaps intimidated by the drive ahead of them. Finally, George's voice broke the silence.

"Is that thing called Boulder Dam or Hoover Dam?"

"I think the government changed it a couple of times," Mike answered from the driver's seat. "Either name works, so how long 'til we're home?"

"Thirteen hours plus the hour lost in the time change," George answered. "Guess we should work some more."

"What do we know about negotiating?" Mike asked.

"I've been doing some work on hostage negotiation techniques," George answered. "That's a tough job."

"Funny how our minds work," Mike responded. "I was thinking of contract negotiations."

"Maybe the same word means the same process," George replied. "Can you remember what we decided about Verbal Judo on Monday or should I read my notes?"

"No, it's clear to me still," Mike said. "So far, we've identified four maxims for Verbal Judo. Though they deal with different kinds of situations, each one is a strategy for taking the other person's point of view and for reasoning from that point of view.

"But there seems a flaw in it to me," Mike continued. "These four strategies all assume that the other person is willing to reason and wants to act for a good purpose, even though their sense of good is different from ours. But some people have different motives from our own, motives so different that we can't figure out what they mean by 'good'. And some people have truly bad motives. Unless Verbal Judo can deflect aggressiveness from those people, its principles will have only limited usefulness."

"You're right," George responded. "We haven't considered how to move people who won't accept social conventions—psychological or physical bullies. We have to test even further."

"I've only seen one instance of negotiation," Mike said, "and it may be too minor an example for our purposes."

"Let me hear it," George said. Then we can decide if it's important or not."

The Encounter

Mike felt a sense of relief as the airplane door closed behind him just as he entered. He was in San Diego, flying once more on business. An early morning meeting that would not end had delayed his arrival at the airport, and he had run desperately through the terminal in order to make his flight.

When he reached the check-in desk three minutes before the 8:30 departure time, only one seat remained in the coach section: a middle seat that faced the bulkhead dividing his section from the first-class section. Under other circumstances he would have been disappointed in so cramped a seat, but today he was relieved simply to have made his flight. He smiled in greeting at the fashionably dressed black woman in the aisle seat next to his, and fastened his seat belt.

The plane had rolled a few feet back from the jetway when it suddenly stopped. After a moment, it moved forward. "Wonder what's wrong?" Mike said to the woman in the aisle seat. "They never go back for good reasons."

"I thought I heard the attendant say that we were going back to pick up a passenger," she said.

"I'm sure that's not possible," Mike responded. "These airlines are more concerned with their schedules that somebody who misses the plane."

"I could be wrong," she said, smiling, "but I work for this line, and they go back for some unexpected reasons."

"They sure never come back for me," Mike said in an exaggerated complaint as the attendant opened the door.

A massive man, dressed for the beach, entered the plane. He turned back to the jetway and filled the front compartment with his booming voice, carrying even through the shriek of the jet engines. "Thank you," he called to the operator, "you're beautiful. I'll never forget this."

He staggered momentarily, nearly dropping the over-stuffed shoulder bag he carried. Then he ricocheted down the empty front compartment. When he reached the last row of first-class seats, those reserved for smokers, he stopped. He unloaded his shoulder bag into the right-hand aisle seat, then dropped the newspapers and books he carried on top of the bag.

At first glance, the large, hairy man seemed out of place on an airplane—and especially misplaced in his class. He wore a gaudy, short-sleeved tropical shirt and rumpled khaki pants. His body was like a bear's, and his wild hair and beard accented the effect.

A closer study suggested another reality. Three of the man's fingers bore delicate, exotic gems set in gold. The watch glimpsed through the hair on his wrist was a jeweled Rolex. His hair and beard had been carefully and professionally curled to look like Bacchus. Even the outrageous shirt, covered with parrots and iridescent palm trees, was no thrift-store bargain. It was hand-sewn, perfectly tailored from original art-deco material.

The man's idiosyncratic dress, combined with the signatures of obvious wealth, identified his special standing in the world of commerce. He was successful enough to ignore the conventions of business and brash enough to create his own iconoclastic style.

After emptying his arms, he slumped into the aisle seat on the left. Mike could see him clearly from his seat behind the bulkhead on the right side of the aircraft.

Despite the fact that every seat in coach was filled the man was the only passenger in first class. The attendant assigned to his section had hurried to him as soon as she had closed the door and had begun storing the items he had dropped in the seat. "Please fasten your seat belt, sir," the attendant said. "We'll be taking off soon."

"I wanna drink," the man said loudly." A Bloody Mary—and make that a double."

"I'm sorry, sir, there won't be time for a drink," the young woman responded. "We'll be taking off very shortly. I'll bring your order as soon as we're airborne."

"Look at that traffic out there," he barked, waving at the line of planes waiting to take off. "We'll be on the ground a long time. Plenty of time for a drink."

Mike and the other coach passengers watched with poorly disguised resentment as the attendant headed for the gallery to prepare the drink. "We'd be at the head of the line if we hadn't gone back for that guy," snorted the man seated at Mike's right.

Mike nodded in agreement, then looked around at his fellow passengers. Except for the woman at his left, the front rows of the coach section were filled with 'frequent

flyers', men in suits flying on business. Most of them had observed the exchange in the first-class section, and each subscribed to a single, if inconsistent, principle: When I fly first class (rare as it may be), I deserve all the attention I can get. When I fly coach, I find first-class passengers unbearable.

"Who do you have to be for them to come back to the gate for you?" Mike asked the woman next to him.

"It depends," she said. "This guy used to play pro football—some sort of lineman. Now he's a scout and road manager for a pro team."

The plane seemed to inch along the taxiway following the line of planes to the end of the runway. Mike noticed that the man in first class was sitting silently, tapping the keys of a small computer that sat on the table in front of him. The flight attendant approached him. "Sir, we're about to take off. You'll need to put your table away now."

"What do you mean 'about to take off?" he snapped. "We won't be first in line for 10 minutes. I'll put the table up in time. Don't worry."

"Sir, the captain has signaled that trays have to be stowed." She gently lifted the small terminal and folded the table into the seat. Then she handed him the computer. "FAA regulations are clear on this point, sir. I'm sorry."

The man cocked his head, and stared at her. "Don't do that again (he stared intently at her breast pocket where a name plate was pinned)… uh, Christine. I'm a 'preferred client', and you better treat me right."

"That's what I'm doing, sir" the attendant said, then walked to the front of the airplane.

"Do you run into many guys like him in your work?" Mike asked the woman in the aisle seat.

"Not a lot," she said, "but enough to have a name for them—attendants call guys like that 'irates.' According to this airline's policy, I could move up to first class now. But I want to stay away from him."

The plane made an awkward pirouette as it turned from the taxiway onto the runway. The sound of the engines building thrust filled the plane, ending conversation. Then the jetliner rumbled down the runway, steadily gaining speed. Finally, the nose lifted and they were airborne.

The plane ascended at an angle that seemed precipitous, pressing its passengers back against their seats. Mike's anxiety about their climb was partially alleviated by his knowledge of Lindbergh Field, which sits on a promontory in San Diego Bay. During departures, planes must climb steeply to escape the surrounding high-rise buildings.

At the apex of the climb Mike stared in disbelief as the irate in first class stood up. The man braced himself against the multiplied force of gravity, opened the storage area above his head, and began to rummage through his shoulder bag.

The flight attendants voice spoke through the intercom: "Please remain in your seats until the captain has turned off the seat-belt sign," it insisted

The man glanced at the flight attendant strapped in

her seat against the cockpit bulkhead. "Don't worry," he called. "I know what I'm doing."

The young woman looked directly at him. Although she was only a few rows away, she spoke again through the intercom. "Sir, please sit down now!"

"Don't talk that way to me," the irate roared." I rack up more bonus miles on this line than most of those turkeys back there (he gestured toward the back of the plane) even fly. Believe me, I know what I'm doing." He turned his attention again to the luggage bin.

The plane's angle of ascent eased as they spoke, and the attendant quickly freed herself from the seat belt and hurried to the standing man. "Sir, you must sit down. I'm sure you know what you're doing. But you are also putting the other passengers at risk."

The irate faced her squarely. "Look, uh, Christine. I book a million and a half bucks a year on this line. Your boss and your boss's boss will notice if I complain. Just let me do what I want to."

"I can't do that sir. If you don't sit down now, I'll be forced to ask the pilot to return to the airport."

The man retrieved an item from the overhead bin and tossed it on the seat beside his. He glared at the attendant and sat down. She immediately closed the storage bin and walked to the galley.

The noise level in the plane subsided as they reached their cruising altitude and headed northeast. The man at Mike's right fell into instant sleep, even before the drink service began. Once the carts appeared in the aisle, a curtain was drawn between the two sections of the aircraft. Mike could still hear the only passenger order Bloody Marys.

"How's the attendant up there doing?" Mike asked the woman in the aisle seat.

"Christine's in a tough spot. An irate like that can put the other passengers at jeopardy. I mean, he must weigh 280 pounds. If we hit an air pocket, he'd be tossed around and could wind up back here, on top of people. But worse than that, he encourages everyone else in the plane to break the rules.

He's violating FAA regulations. We could take him back to San Diego and throw him off the plane. But the company says to be nice to guys who provide that much business, even if they're irates—and he knows it. We're supposed to be understanding and treat them kind of like rude children. He can virtually hold this whole plane full of people hostage to his demands."

They could hear the flight attendant in the front section. "Sir, we don't want you to fly with us again if our service disappoints you," the voice said. "But I'm sure that you'll find that the other lines observe the same regulations as do we. We didn't make these rules."

"You know," the woman at his side said, "passengers never know about the skills and training their attendants have unless there's an emergency. Since they almost never see those skills, most passengers assume that attendants are here to wait on them.

"And we are, I suppose," she continued, smiling. "In simplest terms, we do want to make the customer happy. But there are limits -- set by the federal government and limits defined by our own patience and our resources of good will. We're sort of trapped in the middle, trying to satisfy everybody."

"What options does she have," Mike asked.

"In cases like this, the A-line -- that's what we call the attendant in charge of a flight -- takes over. Christine is the A-line, so that's already happened. The next step is to go to the captain, and that's something attendants try to avoid if at all possible.

"But I'm not worried. If he keeps drinking that much, he'll pass out before we're halfway to Denver."

Mike turned his attention to the breakfast on the tray in front of him, then to a newspaper. He struggled to read as the plane shuddered frequently in the turbulent air. Looking through the window, Mike could see the tops of towering black clouds in the cold winter morning. The warning light above the seat-belt symbol stayed on throughout the flight.

After a while, Mike felt the momentary weightlessness that signaled the plane's initial descent. The charged air buffeted the craft and shook its occupants as the plane knifed into the clouds.

Christine, the flight attendant from the front compartment, opened the curtain and tied it back, revealing the irate sleeping in his seat. Just then a male voice, partly masked by static, emanated from the intercom. "Uh, good morning ladies and gentlemen. This is your first officer speaking. We're now 60 nautical miles from Denver's Stapleton Airport.

"Denver got a foot of snow last night, and the runway has been closed most of the morning. It's open now, but there's still lots of traffic in front of us. We'll be in a holding pattern up here for a little while longer.

"That hold, combined with our late start this morning, means we'll arrive about an hour behind schedule. Those of you hoping to make connecting flights will find that most of them are still on the ground, so you probably will make your flight.

"We'll keep you posted on conditions. The captain asks you to please remain in your seats with your lap belts secured. We're also asking that the flight attendants take their seats. The air may be a bit rough."

Mike felt the plane lurch into a sharp turn. In a few minutes, it turned again, then again, each time to the left. Mike glanced at his watch and estimated that they would make more than 20 such turns if they stayed in the holding pattern for 30 minutes.

The man in first class was suddenly and loudly awake. He jabbed at his call button, staring at the attendant who was strapped against the front bulkhead. When she failed to respond, he rose from his seat and staggered into the rest room.

"Please remain in your seats until we have landed," the woman's voice said over the intercom. The man in first class left the rest room and stopped, facing her. He

steadied himself by gripping seats on each side of the aisle and yelled at her over the straining engines. "Let me talk to the captain!"

"Please take your seat, sir," she said firmly.

"Not until I talk to the pilot," he said. "Tell him this is an emergency."

"I can't interrupt him right now," she answered as the plane again banked to the left. This weather requires the flight crew's undivided attention. Please take your seat and fasten your seat belt."

"This will just take a moment," he insisted. "It's very important."

"I'm sorry. FAA regulations prohibit my opening the door to the cockpit. I do understand that it's important, and if you'll sit down now, I'll come to your seat. Then you can give me exactly what you want me to say to the captain and I'll give him your message over the interphone."

"All right," he said angrily. "But hurry up. This is important."

As soon as he fastened his seat belt, the attendant made her way back to the angry passenger. She sat in the aisle seat opposite his and put her lap belt on. "What would you like me to ask the captain?" she asked.

"Don't ask him. Tell him. Tell him to call the tower and tell them there's an emergency so we can get a priority landing slot."

"Sir, I can't do that," she said calmly. "We don't have an emergency that I'm aware of."

"Look," he rages. "I have to be at a very, very important meeting -- worth a lot of money to me -- in 25 minutes, then I have to fly out of Denver to New York before the afternoon is out. I've got to get on the ground now."

"I can't tell the captain that we have an emergency," she said firmly, "but I'll be happy to describe your problem to the flight crew to see what they can do."

He crossed his arms across his massive chest as she pulled herself to the front of the plane and strapped herself in her seat. She removed the interphone from the cabin wall and spoke into it. After a few minutes she struggled back down the aisle to speak with the man.

"The captain says that he's sorry; but he doesn't feel he can honestly report an emergency."

The large man stood up at her words.

"Please sit down, sir," she said firmly.

He remained standing while he shouted. "I don't care what he feels. This is an emergency. You can tell him that either he gets this plane down now or you can kiss a million and a half bucks goodbye. I'll take our contract to another carrier. And I'll tell every other road manager in the league."

"I'll repeat your message, sir, but only if you sit down and fasten your belt immediately."

The man remained standing for several seconds then slowly sat down. The attendant retraced her treacherous walk up the aisle as the plane once again banked to the left.

"Is this as serious as it looks?" Mike asked the woman at his side.

"It's serious," she said. "Christine doesn't have the authority to do what he wants, but she does have the responsibility to maintain a safe aircraft. She's got to find some middle ground between the customer and policy."

The attendant again retraced her path to the angry man. "Good news, sir. The captain said that he's willing to stretch policy a bit and radio a message ahead for the people you're meeting. I'm sure they'll understand about the weather and wait for you."

"That's not good enough," he said, lurching from his seat. "If I don't get to New York this afternoon, I'm taking my business elsewhere, and I'll tell your management to blame you and your captain."

"Please remain seated, sir," she said calmly. "FAA regulations won't permit you to speak to the captain about personal matters. But even if you could persuade him to request an emergency landing, you'd still miss your meeting and your flight to New York."

The man stared at her, but did not attempt to move to the front of the plane.

"If we make an emergency landing," she went on, "FAA investigators will meet us on arrival. You'll spend the rest of the day answering their questions, and I know they won't be as accommodating as the captain has been."

The large man sank into his seat.

"Let's see if we can figure out your real problem here," she said with a smile. "We do value your business, and we want to help. What time do you need to reach New York?"

The man handed her an itinerary and they studied it together for several minutes.. Then she made her way again to the front of the cabin. Although the intensity of their exchange made the encounter seem lengthy, Mike noted that the plane had been in the holding pattern for only five minutes.

The attendant returned in minutes. "More good news," she said. "We can get you on a 3:30 flight on another airline. You'll get to New York in plenty of time."

"I don't have time to get this ticket rewritten," he complained.

"The captain said he'll make an exception to our policy and ask our agents to make the changes for you. I'm sure you'll be able to keep to your schedule."

"I'll believe it when I see it," he said with a sarcastic chuckle. "Can I get another drink?"

The attendant smiled. "I guess I can get you that without asking the captain. But you'll have to hold it -- your tray has to remain stowed."

The Lesson

"Did he make his flight?" George asked.

"Nope," Mike laughed. "Right after we landed the wind blew up and closed the airport again. But at least he couldn't blame the attendant or the airline."

"That's real negotiation," George said enthusiastically.

"Why?" Mike asked as he drove along the narrow road.

"Think about it in the context of hostage negotiation," George answered. "When someone says 'do this for me or else I'll cause you harm', you have to negotiate, even if you don't like the person and feel outraged by the injustice of the demands.

"The negotiator is the person in the middle, mediating between the two adversaries. And that's where the attendant was. She had to strike a middle ground between the extremes of the customer's demands and the inflexibility of the airline's policies."

"I suppose that's true," Mike responded, "but the rest of the people in the plane would rather that they hadn't compromised with him."

"Sure," George said, "and the judgments those observers make complicate the negotiation process. But when people have real power, you have to give up something to get a satisfactory resolution. The fact that he was so aggressive and that he did have big money to use as a threat made him a real problem one that couldn't be ignored, even if the people who do abide by the rules were upset.

"The essential condition of negotiation is that you have to give up something to get something. The captain acting for the airline had to do something extraordinary. He was forced to violate some policies."

"I guess I don't see an alternative to his actions," Mike said, "but I still have a sense of resentment about it. If the captain was making the decisions, what role did the attendant play?"

"She had to be the actual negotiator," George said. "And negotiators can't have the power to give anything up themselves."

"Why is that important?"

"Negotiators can only convey offers and counter-offers. That prevents the person who is threatening from attacking the negotiator personally. See, on that flight, the guy was forced to regard her as someone who can help him, not an adversary.

"So, what happened is that he could no longer see her as an enemy and he started to treat her as a vehicle for communication -- as a way to get his point across. And that forced him to think about the means for achieving his purpose, not the goal itself."

"But doesn't that give too much power to people like that?" Mike asked.

"Yes and no," George responded. "There are limits in all negotiations.

"In the case of the airline, the limits were clear. They couldn't allow blackmail. The captain wouldn't break regulations and he wouldn't jeopardize the safety of the passengers. But within those limits he did make special efforts to placate a belligerent and valued customer. That's why they went back for him in the first place, and that's why they broke some internal policies to keep him happy."

"But that seems to say that only the airline had to observe limits," Mike complained. "That guy wasn't limited in what he would do."

"Not so," George said. "People negotiate because they do face limits. He couldn't jump out of the plane, or land it himself. And he didn't want to get caught up in an investigation. If he pushed too hard, the airline did have lots of administrative pressure it could bring.

"So what happened is that the captain -- through the attendant -- tried to give him what he needed, not what he thought he wanted. And that resolved the crisis."

"Is that the sort of balance police try to reach in hostage negotiation?" Mike asked.

"Exactly," George answered. "The police have to protect the safety of the hostages. They could do that by giving in. But they also have to maintain the law as well as the larger context of law and order. They can't give in or they'll lose credibility as a force for social order.

"They have to hold a line, even while they give up some ground. And that's what went on during your flight.

"And one more thing. People who seize power -- like a

criminal with hostages -- get pretty abusive. And someone like that guy who plays pro ball has been rewarded his whole life for being aggressive. But the negotiator can't react personally to insults or the focus of the exchange falls on personality, not on the goal.

"In those terms," Mike said thoughtfully, "these conditions apply to labor negotiations. The Harvard negotiating team says that the goal of negotiation is to 'get to yes' and they described the process as negotiation jujitsu."

"That sounds a lot like Verbal Judo," George said.

"It is. They say that you first have to 'read' the other person, respond to his or her reasoning process, and then attempt to fashion a mediated position, one somewhere between the other's first demand and your first reaction."

"The art of negotiation seems the same in all these cases," George concluded. "We have to find a middle ground to reach a resolution."

"That's right," Mike responded, "We're looking for a ground on which real business can be done. That's what 'negotiation' first meant, after all -- doing business. And you can't do business unless you can get to that middle."

"Strange as it seems," George remarked, "the process reminds me of a throw in judo called tomoe nage—a 'stomach throw'."

"How's that?" Mike asked with a laugh.

"Tomoe nage is especially effective when my opponent is extremely aggressive and comes right at me. The throw allows the attacker to go in the direction he wants initially, while I give way. But by giving way, I control his direction and momentum."

"Explain."

"As my opponent comes at me, I stay in place rather than side stepping or resisting. When he starts to push or grab me, I simply bend my knees -- almost like sitting down on the ground. But while I'm doing it, I place one foot right in the middle of his stomach.

"As his momentum comes forward, I control and direct him by bringing him up and over with my leg as I roll backward. I give way in order to control."

"That sounds like negotiation," Mike said.

"It does," George went on, "but there's more. My foot has to be positioned exactly in the middle of his abdomen for the throw to work. If I'm too high, he won't go over me and will remain standing above me -- he'll have the advantage.

"But if my foot's too low, he'll fall on top of me, and we'll start grappling without purpose or control."

"Sounds like a good metaphor. Do you have a principle for Verbal Judo?"

"It seems pretty obvious to me."

Give way in order to control.

"That's helpful," Mike said. "It gives us a way to deal with belligerent people whom we can't reason with."

"Well, that will work with some belligerent people," George responded, "but there are situations where it won't work."

"Let's take that up later," Mike answered. "We're almost back to Kingman and the interstate. Want to take one more drive down Andy Devine Boulevard?"

"I'll pass," George said with a laugh. "Let's get some gas and keep moving."

7

The Language of Reassurance

The Challenge

"We'll get to Flagstaff in an hour and a half George said. "I want to stop here. I almost took a teaching job there once."

"You mean at Northern Arizona State? I've seen the school," Mike said. "It's a pretty campus. By the way, I've been thinking about that experience I had on the plane, and the principles of negotiation that we talked about."

"Tell me," George said.

"Well, as tense as the situation seemed to me in the plane, no real harm was likely—just lost pride or money," Mike spoke slowly, thinking while he talked. "But what if negotiation hadn't worked and the guy got so irate that he lost control?"

"Those are limits that I didn't see before," George answered. "We have to find ways to use Verbal Judo that don't depend on being rational. So far, every tactic we've

discussed relied on some form of 'reasoning'. But that can't always work.

"Consider this question for a minute: How can the appeal of Verbal Judo work if the other person is so frustrated by the situation that he or she is incapable of acting reasonably, let alone responding to appeals to reason? People who are hurt or angry often think that no one cares. They get frustrated and they lose the ability to be reasonable."

"You're right about that," Mike answered. "Words often have little impact on people who are upset by pain or are overcome by grief. But I shouldn't have to remind you that this whole idea started with your desire to develop a metaphor from judo.

"Besides, even I have seen unreasonable people calmed with words."

"That's what I need," George said. "Talk!"

The Encounter

The heavy glass doors withdrew to each side as if in alarm as Mike approached the entrance marked ADMITTING, PATIENT INFORMATION. Although he sought none of these services, he knew nowhere else within the sprawling hospital complex to look. A call from a friend had brought him in search of the Emergency Room.

Although it was after 9:00 p.m. on a Friday, the confusion in the parking area was overwhelming. Once inside the lobby, Mike became even more disoriented. Cautiously, he approached a raised, round desk in the center of the room where a woman sat. Before her was an array of buttons and lights that controlled telephone connections throughout the complex of buildings.

"Excuse me," he said in a raised whisper.

"Yes," the woman responded without inflection, scarcely glancing at him.

"Perhaps you can help me. I'm trying to locate a friend of mine who is being treated here. His name is Gregory Pines."

Her hands moved rapidly across a keyboard, and she gazed intently at the screen in front of her. "He hasn't been admitted. Try EE ARE," the woman said curtly. Then she turned back to the console to satisfy its beeping and flashing.

Not certain he had understood her, Mike asked a young man in an orderly's uniform. The youth pointed toward closed double doors. "Through those doors, turn at the Radiology Lab, then go through the hall that says Medical Staff Only, and take the elevator down to the rear street level. After you get off the elevator, turn left, and go to the end of the corridor. That's it."

He set out according to his instructions. As he walked along the halls, he noticed that several doors stood open. Whenever he passed an open door, he felt torn. On the one hand, his compelling curiosity tempted him to look in at the patients lying on their beds. At the same time, he did not want to be impolite by staring at another's suffering,

and he tried to avoid eye contact.

His confusion persisted as he made his way tentatively through the winding halls, for he sensed that he was out of place. Men and women, clad in crisply starched white uniforms or shapeless coveralls of greenish-gray, filed past him with purposeful frenzy.

At last, confused and tense, he found the doors marked EMERGENCY ROOM.

He went through the doors and stopped at an open window where a young woman sat at a typewriter. "Do you need emergency services, sir?" she asked.

"No, he answered with a sense of relief. "I'm trying to locate a man who is being treated here. His name is Gregory Pines."

The young woman leafed through a stack of papers. "Oh, yes," she said cheerfully. "He's in X-ray now. Won't you take a chair in the Waiting Room?"

He followed her pointing finger to a large room filled with plastic and steel chairs. About half the seats held people whose posture and expression revealed their pain and confusion. Those waiting had taken chairs far from one another, choosing to endure the wait in solitude. All seemed tense and impatient. A young woman tried vainly to quiet her baby, while, in another part of the room an aged man watched the events around him apprehensively.

Just as he had selected the most isolated seat he turned and caught sight of a large man, his face flushed, talking aloud to himself: "I won't wait another hour!"

The man's face revealed the pain he felt. The man's left arm hung uselessly at his side … a shoulder separation, Mike concluded. He noted the loose-fitting white jacket and the calluses on the sides of the man's hands. "Probably injured in a fight," he imagined. Whether the encounter was a street battle or a sanctioned meet, Mike could not know, but he wondered when the man's anger would explode into action.

As the minutes passed, the man's angry muttering continued. Mike watched him cautiously, then turned to survey the room. It was then he caught sight of a nurse moving from one person to another. She was dressed in a white uniform and cap; over her shoulders she wore an unbuttoned, pale-blue sweater. Her hair was almost entirely gray but he was sure she was no more than 50 years old. An embossed piece of plastic that she wore identified her as Rosemary Wilson. She seemed to hear the muttered curses and approached the angry man without hesitation. "Is there something I can do to help you?" she asked warmly.

"You can't help me but that doctor over there could," he exploded, pointing with his good arm in the direction of a bearded man in surgical coveralls who could be seen down one of the corridors. "None of you seem to be concerned that people are hurt out here. I've been here for more than 45 minutes, and no one seems ready to…"

"Let me see if I understand you," she interrupted, taking out a note pad. "You've been here for almost an hour, is that right?"

"Yeah," he said, "and…"

"Please, let me make sure I get this right," she interrupted gently. "And during that time, you feel that no one has tried to help you. You must think that you're being ignored while we do other things that don't help your shoulder."

"They told me they had to call a doctor in to operate on my shoulder. Why can't he do it?" The man gestured angrily down the hall.

"That's Dr. Averham," she responded. "He's assigned to Treatment and Admitting this evening and, I'm afraid, can't help you."

"But why?" he snarled. "I've been here an hour, and he hasn't seemed very busy to me. Now I hear that I have to wait another hour for some or-tho-pe-dic surgeon." He bit off the syllables as he said them.

"Yes, Dr. Gernright. I'm sure you find that an unnecessary delay. How frustrated you must feel," she answered.

"I'm glad someone figured that out," he snapped back. "But why do I have to sit out here and wait?"

"I want to assure you that we are doing everything we can. Dr. Gernright is one of our best orthopedic surgeons. He was located at a dinner party with friends, and he gave up his evening out as soon as we reached him. I know that he is hurrying here even now.

"But this whole process must seem thoughtless to you, since a doctor is right down the hall. Still, strange as it seems, Dr. Averham is doing his job, which is to be constantly prepared for life-threatening situations and other emergencies. If he were to begin your surgery and an emergency occurred, he would be unprepared and, worse, might have to leave you on the operating table while he attended to it."

The man, now slumped in his chair, shuddered visibly at the suggestion of interrupted surgery. "But the pain in my shoulder is terrible, and no one seems to care."

"I know that you're in pain, and we do want to help you in every way that we can. How were you hurt?"

"I was sparring—I do karate." he responded.

That's a very rough sport," she said. "Have you been injured in other fights?"

"Nothing like this. The pain is killing me."

"I'm sure it hurts," she said, touching his good shoulder sympathetically, "but you're in excellent condition. I doubt that the pain could kill someone of your build."

He smiled belligerently.

"Would you like some aspirin?" she asked.

"I never touch any of that stuff," he snapped. "I only came here because my friends insisted. Then they left."

"I'm very impressed that you can endure pain so bravely. I guess that's what I'm asking you to do now, to endure a little longer—to continue acting bravely. I know that you want to let off steam, but your anger is frightening people who need all the reassurance they can get.

"I know that your shoulder hurts now," she went on, "but I'll bet you'll be back in competition in a few months. Try to remember, though, that some people here have suffered permanent injuries. They need quiet and calm around them. Can I ask you to bear up a little longer? You have my personal guarantee of help as soon as it is possible."

The man said nothing, but his face revealed that he would not again cause a disturbance.

"Thank you," the nurse said quietly. "I'll be back in a few minutes. I do appreciate your understanding and patience."

She walked to the open window where the young woman sat. "I'm going down to the cafeteria for some coffee, Julie," Mike heard her say. "Be back in 15 minutes."

Mike interrupted her as she started down the hall. "May I walk with you and ask you some questions?" he asked. "I'd like to know more about the approaches you use when working with people in distress."

She looked at him inquisitively. "I don't mean to intrude," he went on, "but I teach people who work in stressful situations and they often ask me how to do what you just did. Can you give me any suggestions?"

The nurse smiled. "You tell me—what's your impression of this place?"

"Chaos," he responded forcefully.

"And that chaos makes you feel anxious, threatened, and alienated. Am I right?

"Yes," he answered, only now relaxing from the encounter he had just witnessed.

The nurse went on. "Those of us who work here take that chaos for granted. Like my old college roommate who was working at the American Hospital in Beirut at the time of the civil strife, we develop a siege mentality that allows us to accept as routine what everyone else finds personally threatening. My old roommate used to say when she called, 'Stop worrying! The shelling is at least half a mile away.'

"And we not only take this orderly chaos for granted, we know policies and procedures so well that we repeat them in our sleep. But many of the people we have to deal with experience this place only once in their whole lives. We seat them out in the Waiting Room, knowing much more about their real physical condition than they do themselves. Think of it. I see two, maybe three separations a week, but I'll bet that this is a first for 'Bruce Lee' back there."

They walked along the deserted service line in the cafeteria. Mike waited as she filled two oversize Styrofoam cups and pressed covers on them.

I guess what we do is forget to empathize," she continued as they left the cafeteria. "What we see when we look at the Waiting Room is 'an orderly priority of care based on pragmatic diagnoses of medical urgency'—that's what it says in the book. What those people see is some terrible dance of death—like in the Middle Ages.

"They watch somebody moaning in the corner, and they worry that person has something infectious. Next to them

sits a dangerous-looking male from a minority they don't trust, wrapped in bandages with blood seeping out.

"And they're convinced we don't care that they are in pain. Einstein was right, you know. Time is relative; when you're in pain, the minutes do pass more slowly.

"So they become frustrated, and they react in the only way they can, trying to get our attention, trying to say, 'Can't you understand? I need help. Please do something.' But of course they don't actually say that. They explode at us.

"I can't change those medical priorities. But I can help them by providing a perspective that will sustain them during their wait."

"It's not that hard to do," she responded. "When he insisted that no one cared, I let him express his frustration. I listened instead of taking it personally or defending our policies. I had to resist letting his tenseness make me tense. People who are tense are self-centered—they want to get rid of their tension. If I start worrying about my own tension, I can't pay attention to his.

"Then once I persuaded him that I was listening, I tried to paraphrase his words. I've found that even people who are highly agitated will listen to me when I repeat what they said."

"That's been my experience also" Mike said.

"Well," she went on, "once he stopped snarling and began listening, I could help him by taking his point of view. Once we shared the same perspective, he calmed down quickly. That injury must have taken a lot out of him.

"But that approach won't work with everybody," she went on. "He's a tough guy, and I tried to appeal to that in him. In other situations, I'll try to figure out as much as I can about each patient and respond individually.

"For example, when I have to calm someone out there who is paralyzed by grief, I let them know that they can count on me to be stable and controlled. If they're ready, I'll try to give practical suggestions about what has to be done and how to go about doing it.

"And when I encounter fear, I do everything I can to build confidence and to explain what will happen in the future."

They arrived at the entrance to the Emergency Room. "Do you ever use these techniques with the doctors and other staff members here?" Mike asked.

Ms. Wilson smiled. "My break is over now. I hope I've been able to be of some help."

"Thanks so much for your help," Mike said and walked into the Waiting Room. He watched as the karate man was helped into a wheelchair, then went back to the desk to inquire about his friend.

"Mr. Pines has been admitted for an appendectomy, sir," the young woman said. "You won't be able to see him until tomorrow between 2 and 4:30 p.m."

"Is there some way to find out how he is?" Mike asked anxiously.

"My records indicate only that he is in pre-op. You'll have to call his personal physician tomorrow morning to get more information."

"Who's his doctor?" Mike asked.

"I'm sorry sir," she answered. "I can't give out that information."

Mike turned from the window, anxious about his friend and frustrated at the wasted trip to the hospital. Then he left the building at the street level amidst the ambulances and the jumble of hastily parked cars.

The Lesson

"I think I've found my answer," George noted from the passenger's seat. "Using Verbal Judo can reassure people who are distraught beyond reason. Your Nurse Wilson called it 'empathy', and I think she's right."

"Let me play devil's advocate," Mike answered. "Think about it for a moment. Isn't empathy familiar enough without our having to make it into a principle?"

"It's familiar, and yet it isn't," George answered. "Most people—and I have been one of them—confuse empathy with 'sympathy', but the meaning is very different. Empathy does not mean that we feel for the other person, it means we feel like them. And that means we have to see the world through their eyes and feel the emotional stress they have felt. Until then, we can't really help them.

"But you can't help them if you share their distress and get caught up in it," George continued. "Empathy is like Dr. Kano's principle of the still-center. We can't act for others unless we ourselves are calm."

"But can empathy be a tactic for Verbal Judo?" Mike asked. "Or is it only a state of mind?

"I am certain that we've learned a new principle of Verbal Judo," George said. "The alteration of behavior you witnessed in that hospital is similar to a counter-throw I use called ushiro gushi, a 'reverse hip throw'. I usually use that throw when my opponent is out of control and attacking wildly.

"When people are overwrought, they get an extra shot of adrenaline, and they're stronger and less predictable than under normal circumstances. The only way you can control them is to keep in very close contact and to maintain your own balance and equilibrium. You have to absorb their excess energy and redirect that explosive force so they don't overwhelm you."

"That sounds a lot easier than it probably is to actually do," Mike said skeptically.

"Not really," George said. "If you want the specifics, the throw goes this way. When my opponent rushes at me, I lower my center of gravity, and encircle his waist with both arms to contain the negative energy. Then I arch my body backwards. That movement lifts the other person off the ground, and neutralizes his strength. I can then actually guide him to the ground using whatever force I need."

"I think I understand," Mike responded. "In ushiro goshi you absorb the person's wild energy and lead him to a harmless position."

"Right," George went on. "And that's why I feel that this move is like empathy. You don't want to deny the negative energy that people feel. They're upset, and they want help. But you can't let their explosiveness threaten others. So you paraphrase their words—you put their thoughts into your words—to absorb their frustration, and then you can move them to act less destructively."

"Can you state it as a principle of Verbal Judo?" Mike asked.

"Absolutely," George answered.

Use empathy to absorb tension.

"I like it," Mike went on. "But I need a break and I need lunch. Besides, you may want to job-hunt in Flagstaff. Let's turn off up here."

8

The Language of Enforcement

The Challenge

"We could go to the Grand Canyon," George said, pointing to the sign that marked the exit. They were leaving the eastern limits of Flagstaff with half their drive yet ahead of them. "Wish we didn't have to make that presentation tomorrow."

"No choice about that one," Mike said. "Besides, I'm still working on Verbal Judo."

"What are we missing?" George asked.

"Well, the situations on the plane and in the hospital were very tense," Mike replied, "but the potential for real violence wasn't very high. Sometimes people have to confront a real threat of physical harm. Can Verbal Judo work when people are prepared to resort to force? Wouldn't that sort of threat invalidate what you're calling Verbal Judo?"

"I don't think so," George answered. "Even before I became a cop, I saw police use words in threatening

situations. I'm sure that Verbal Judo can indicate a way to respond to physically threatening situations."

"You haven't told me about how you got started in police work," Mike said. "I'd love to hear."

"I didn't set out to join the force," George answered. "I went out as a ride-along because I was interested in what police actually do on the streets."

"You talk, I'll take notes," Mike said.

The Encounter

George recalled waiting nervously at the rear of the squad room before his first ride-along in a police car. He listened while the shift sergeant completed his instructions to the night shift. He had received a complete description of the officer he would ride with, a patrolman named Bruce McFair. The officer was leaning back in a metal folding chair, taking notes. After the sergeant dismissed the squad, Officer McFair walked quickly over to him, holding out his hand.

"Hi. You must be my guest for the evening," the uniformed man said.

"Yes," George said, returning the handshake.

"I hope you don't mind if we chat as we walk. I've got to get into service. Saturday nights are usually pretty tough duty."

As they drove through the downtown city streets, George spoke enthusiastically. "I've heard you hold advanced belts in a few different martial arts. I've studied judo, karate, and a few other techniques over much of my life as well, but I haven't been in many situations where I could actually use it. But you must find plenty of use for your judo out here."

"I don't want to disappoint you, George, but I rarely throw anyone. I find that words are my most powerful force option."

"What do you mean words as a 'force option'? What..." He broke off the question as the car accelerated.

"We've got a call," Bruce said.

"How did you know the radio was calling for you? All I hear is noise."

"Selective attention. It's the first thing you learn out in one of these cars. You hear what you should hear."

The officer moved rapidly through a corner while switching on his overhead lights. "We've got a disturbance in the alley behind this street."

As the officer pulled into the dark alley, he could see two men thrusting at each other. With the car's arrival, the smaller man fled while the very large man turned to face the advancing headlights. George noticed a shiny object in his right hand—a broken quart beer bottle.

"Watch this guy, Bruce. He's got a weapon."

George felt a rush of adrenalin as the car stopped sharply. He fought numberless times in sanctioned bouts, but he had never tested his skills on the streets. He estimated the large man's size rapidly—perhaps 6'7", 250 pounds—and determined the throws he would use. As he seized his door handle, however, Bruce's whispered command stopped him: "Stay in the car, George. I'll deal with this—department policy says you can only observe."

He sank back in disappointment as Bruce picked up his cap from the car seat. "Okay," he sighed. "I'll wait and listen." Through the windshield, he could see the events play out in front of him as if on a stage, illuminated by the squad car's headlights.

Bruce walked into the circle of light towards the agitated man. Suddenly, the man lifted his arm above his head and yelled drunkenly, "Hey, pig, stay the hell away from me. You want trouble I'll give you all you want!"

Bruce paused in his advance, took half a step back and leaned even further back in an even, almost conversational tone. "I just got a call that there was some kind of disturbance, probably a fight going on back here. Do you think they meant you and your friend?" Bruce gestured in the direction of the fleeing man.

"Yeah, pig, that's him. And you're next if you give me any trouble. I'll walk right over you. You're nothing. You're not taking me, Jack. I've had enough of you pigs."

"Hey, I believe it," the uniformed man responded evenly. "I can see that you're big enough, and probably as tough as they come. I don't need that kind of trouble."

"Officer, I want to press charges against that man." The voice from behind the car surprised the ride-along, although the officer apparently had anticipated the man's arrival. The man entered the circle of light and stood across from the object of his anger, partially screened by Bruce. "I want that man in jail. He and his biker friends trashed my place, broke a couple tables, and scared away my paying customers."

"Sorry, friend," Bruce said slowly, still addressing the giant wielding the broken bottle. "It looks like I've got to take you in. This man is signing a complaint against you, and the law says I've got no choice but to arrest you. Why don't you do this the smart way? Put that bottle down and come with me peacefully."

"You're not big enough or tough enough to take me, Jack! Come on, try it."

The man advanced three clumsy steps toward the officer. Watching from the car George was certain that Bruce would use a quick, brutal takedown to end the threat. Instead, Bruce moved three steps back and assumed a defensive posture.

"Wait a minute. Just wait a minute. I know that you can come right through me. No problem. I'll give you that. And those sirens you can hear coming? Well, I know who my backup guys are, and you can probably take them too.

"It might even take ten guys to put you down. But, my man, that tenth patrolman will bring you down, because the law gives us no choice, even if we wanted one. You are going to jail.

"Think of it this way," the uniformed man went on. "Right now you're facing, at the most, a disorderly conduct rap—and that's if they can prove it. But you swing on me, punch me and a couple other officers around, and instead of a $30 conviction, you'll be looking at $500 and 90 days in jail.

"You can do what you want, but it seems to me that your choices are the chance of a $30 fine or a guaranteed conviction for assault and battery on a police officer. That will take you out of circulation, out of work, and out of money for a long time. Maybe you got that kind of money, that kind of time. Maybe you don't. Think about it."

The officer took a step toward the angry man, who raised the bottle higher. "Hell, it just might be worth it to take a few of you all down before you get me."

"Sure, I can see that," Bruce went on evenly. "If you really think it'll make you feel good, do it. Just be sure you don't make the wrong choice."

McFair paused while the man struggled to think clearly through his alcoholic haze. "You do work, don't you?" he continued. "Got some money coming in, maybe a good woman who waits up for you? That all might be there for you in six months, but that's the chance you take if you beat me up. Is that kind of grief worth it?"

The man's flushed face looked pensive. "You've got a point there, pig. You're sure as hell not worth the hassle. I need the bread more than I need to beat you up. But I know I could take you."

"No question about it," the uniformed man said with a smile. "Now, why don't you drop that bottle, let me slip the cuffs on you real quick, and we'll get outta here. Those other cars are about a block away—no need to mess with them. Why not go easy on yourself?"

"Yeah, okay, this time," the subject said quietly, dropping the bottle at his feet. "Next time, me and you might just go a round or two, when I haven't been drinking so much."

George watched in amazement as the man walked to the car and placed his hands on the hood. He still felt angry and frustrated that Bruce had given up so easily, but he held his objections inside himself.

The remainder of the night and early morning hours were filled with numerous encounters—most with drunk drivers—but Bruce was not challenged again. After the shift had ended, they sat drinking coffee in a small restaurant as the early morning sun rose.

George could contain his irritation no longer. "Bruce, I don't understand why you gave in out there. You let that drunk have the victory without a confrontation. I know what he didn't know—that you have the training to dispose of him easily had he attacked. He had a high center of gravity and he was way too aggressive. A power body-drop throw, like tai otoshi, would have put him out for hours, right?"

"Probably, noted Bruce, but remember anything can happen in an alley. I hope you also noticed the outcome of the encounter?"

"Well, the man is in jail," George conceded. "But didn't you lose face with the subject, and with that bartender?"

"I don't want to be critical, but that attitude gets people hurt all the time. And not just suspects—innocent bystanders and officers are hurt and killed because the cop has to 'save face'. Consider confrontation in those terms then tell me what you observed."

"Well, George answered slowly, "You complimented that man and still did your duty. You got him to comply without having to use your physical skill or strength."

"I do try to move with the subject's sense of himself rather than resist it, to get him to do what is in everyone's best interest no matter what might be said."

"I'm fascinated," George responded. "Are all members of your department so skillful and thoughtful in their use of words?"

"No, I'm afraid not," Officer McFair replied, "not many, anyway. Most of them still think that being hard-nosed and forceful is enough. But I don't think so. In my earliest courses at the Police Academy, we learned that all cops have five 'force options' when they encounter resistance.

"The first option, unless we enter the situation under fire, is the use of words. The second one—the one you know best—is 'empty hand' control. Third is a 'chemical' option, like Mace. Fourth is the stick or baton and last, of course, is the revolver.

"Now, we've got five choices," Bruce continued slowly, "but think of the problems created by using any of the last four if they are not absolutely necessary. Torn uniforms, tons of paperwork, explanations to review boards, formal and informal complaints, even liability suits.

"If I break someone's arm or wrist, he'll sue the department as well as me. The stick is also a deadly weapon in the hands of a well-trained officer. The more deadly the force option the more complaints and the closer the public's scrutiny and involvement."

"But surely force is often necessary," George said. "You deal with some very tough people out here, some who actually enjoy hurting people or even taking another's life."

"Absolutely," Bruce resumed. "Those who endanger the lives of others, or those who combine aggressive actions with aggressive words and violate my personal danger zone, must be dealt with forcibly. Every officer has to be prepared to use force in situations like that.

"But those things are a lot less common than most people, and most police officers, think. One study I read by the federal government shows that only three percent of all police encounters require physical force. All the rest are handled—or should be handled—with words.

"The art of police work, as far as I'm concerned, lies in selecting the most appropriate force option for the situation. Police officers call it the 'doctrine of selective force', and the good ones know how to choose the lowest option necessary and how to escalate to the other options.

"I constantly remind myself of the usefulness of words as a force option. The 'martial art of words' is what I call it. Too many of my colleagues tend to see words and verbal strategies as only 'icing on the cake' or 'public relations B.S.'. But the ones who are street savvy know that the

mind and the mouth make mighty antagonists against those who are prepared to use violence."

"Bruce, I'm sure that you're right," George responded. "But don't you find it embarrassing to give in to thugs like that guy?"

"I don't see it as 'giving in'," the officer answered. "I've been on the streets for more than a couple of years and in all that time I've never run into a subject who says to me, 'Hey, I know I'm being unreasonable, but I'm still going to punch this guy out.' They all believe—every one of them—that they're acting reasonably and that I'm the unreasonable one. In their minds, in the context of the events that they know, I guess that they're right."

"You have an interesting way of approaching people who don't agree with you," George said.

"It's interesting, yes," replied Bruce. "But it reflects also the bottom-line assumption that I make every time I confront someone who is hostile or who is prone to violence. I force myself to see the event—whatever it may be—through the eyes of the subject. If I can understand his sense of 'reasonable', no matter how unreasonable I may know it to be; I can better move or direct him towards a mutually acceptable sense of reasonableness."

"Is that what you did with that guy in the alley?" George asked.

"Yeah, I guess so. He saw himself as 'King of the Mountain' in that alley, and I let him have that point. After all, I can't afford to see every encounter as a personal matter; when I'm on duty I represent society, not myself.

"So I let him see himself as he wanted to. All I did was redirect his 'reasoning' to see the full consequences of all the options. Since he didn't feel threatened by me directly, he was capable of considering the economic and personal arguments.

"I might have lost a little—call it 'personal face'—but I did save my 'professional face'. I saved myself, the public, and even that gorilla a lot of time and trouble. I figure I'm doing a good job."

George stood up as Bruce pushed back from the table. "Have to get home," the uniformed man said. "It may be 7:30 in the morning, but I'm heading for bed. Let me know if you'll be signing up for reserve training. I'd love to work on some self-defense moves with you."

"I will. You've taught me a lot, Bruce," George said as they shook hands. "I hope I can return the favor someday." He sat down again as the officer walked out into the harsh morning sun.

The Lesson

"That's a heavy story," Mike said. "Did you use McFair's tactics when you were on the street?"

"All the time," George answered. "Now I'd be inclined to call it Verbal Judo."

"My uncle was a cop, and a tough one," Mike said. "He would probably have been critical of that approach. I'll bet McFair's explanation surprised you."

"It did, and it didn't," George said. "I was disturbed at first, but I did see both the value in it and the courage such a tactic takes. And McFair's attitude may be what we have missed all along in trying to estimate judo's power to do good in the modern world."

"How's that?" Mike asked.

"During all the years I was in training and in tournament play," George explained, "I believed that the best defense was a good attack. And I believe that is still true for tournaments.

"But a police officer's job," he went on, "by its very definition, is to act for the good of others, to preserve peacefulness and order despite the apparent chaos caused by society's outlaws. What I witnessed showed how one person transforms the principles of physical judo into tactics that create voluntary compliance with society's goals. And he does so at the risk of personal embarrassment."

"I'll grant that, Mike said. "But did you watch one man's talent or did you learn a principle for enforcement? What is McFair's principle for action?"

"He does have a principle," George answered. "It's much like Dr. Kano's principle," George answered. "It's much like Dr. Kano's principle of Soft Overcomes Hard. Officer McFair absorbs the aggression directed at him and, in that way, removes the threat.

"In some ways, his street principle is like the first counter-throw that I learned years ago, yoko guruma. My Master told me then that the move required me to 'give way in order to control'.

"The move begins like ushiro goshi—the throw I described to you before we got to Flagstaff," he said, twisting in his seat. "When an attacker comes at me, I lower my center of gravity, encircle his waist with my arms, and step over his left leg, placing my leg between his. As I do this, I begin to twist, pulling the attacker with both arms. By moving in the same direction the attacker is trying to make me move, the force created by gravity's pull on my body will bring both of us down. But I know where and how I want to land and so I can stay in control.

"McFair's tactic also relies on the basic principle of physical judo that of using the other's force to complete your throw rather than resisting and trying to overpower.

"In fact," he went on, "when McFair faces a hostile and antagonistic subject, he finds that the most effective countering technique is to move in the same direction as the subject. He calls it 'moving with the other's sense of reasonableness'."

Mike interrupted and went on with the interpretation. "So, in Ushiro Goshi you first absorb the other's force and then guide him to a harmless position. In yoko guruma, on the other hand, you absorb the opponent's force and use it against him. The subject is allowed to express his own energy, even while the officer stays in control and forces the subject to act in more socially acceptable ways."

"Exactly," George responded. "Bruce first called his technique 'the martial art of words', but I think he'll like Verbal Judo better, once I give him the phrase."

"Better and better, my friend," Mike laughed. "How would you state our new principle of Verbal Judo?"

"I'd use Dr. Kano's words."

Overcome hard with soft.

"We just may have something here," Mike said enthusiastically. "But I need to stop driving for a few minutes—all I can see in the rearview mirror is the sun. Let's pull off at this rest stop and we can watch it set on the Painted Desert."

"Is this the Painted Desert?" George asked in surprise. "I guess I expected more vivid colors," he added, looking out at the pastel surroundings. "Maybe the sunset will brighten it up."

9

The Language of Punishment

The Challenge

As they pulled off the highway into the rest area, Mike saw only two cars, parked close together, in front of the rest rooms.

As Mike drove toward the cars, a beefy man wearing a dark suit, white shirt, and black tie stepped from one of the big sedans. He held his arm up, his broad palm facing them in a command to halt. Mike stopped and rolled his window down. The man leaned toward the window, a laminated identification card in his hand.

"Good evening, gentlemen," he said, offering the card for a distant inspection. "I'm a United States Marshal on official business. I'll have to ask you to park over there," he said, gesturing toward the truck parking area. "You'll be free to use the facilities in a few minutes."

"Whatever you say, officer," Mike said seriously. He glanced at the small brick building as he pulled away and

noticed two more heavily built men—both dressed in dark suits—standing before the door marked MEN.

Mike parked where he had been instructed, and George and he watched over their shoulders. They stared as yet another suited man emerged from the rest room and held the door open. One of the two waiting outside nodded at him, and he called back into the building.

A man emerged from the room wearing a white denim jumpsuit. His hands were clutched tightly at his stomach, drawing his shoulders forward so that he stood in a slightly stooped position. He shuffled into the sunset rather than walked. "That guy's shackled," George said.

Two more men in suits followed from the rest room and took up positions on either side and slightly behind the chained man. Then they began a curious procession toward the cars, with the unshackled men carefully matching the pace of the man they surrounded.

As they reached one of the cars, the marshal who had directed them to their parking spot opened the rear door. The circle of lawmen helped the prisoner into the rear seat of the car, making special efforts to protect his head from the car roof.

Once the door had closed behind the prisoner, the marshals seemed to relax. George and Mike waited in their car, not knowing what signal would indicate that they could leave their car. Several of the dark-suited men lighted cigarettes and each, in turn, made the walk to the rest room. They remained no more than five minutes, then they stepped into the cars. The sedan carrying the prisoner pulled away first, followed closely by the second car filled with officers.

"What do you make of that?" Mike asked.

"Probably a prisoner being transferred," George answered knowledgeably. "But it's hard to say where they're heading."

"I suppose that's the limit for Verbal Judo," Mike said as they stepped out of the car into the evening desert chill. "All the tactics that we've discussed rest on an appeal to some good or reasonable quality in the other person. But there are bad people, people outside the norms of ethics and values that we've discussed. If you can't redirect behavior to positive ends, you have to punish people."

"That's right," George responded. "But people have to observe the principles of Verbal Judo, even when punishing someone, or they will mistake their role. Whenever you punish another, you have to maintain an attitude of disinterest rather than express your anger or frustration."

"Do you think people in the prison system would agree with you?" Mike "asked. "Isn't it hard to keep an emotional distance when you're dealing with people who commit terrible crimes?"

"That's when disinterest is especially important," George answered. "I learned that when I worked at a prison."

"I forgot that you had some first-hand experience," Mike said. "Tell me what that was like."

The Encounter

A year prior to their trip, George had traveled to a medium security prison in the southwest to discuss revisions in the institution's training curriculum. On his arrival, however, he learned that the superintendent who had invited him was tied up with an emergency.

While he waited for the superintendent, a young correctional officer gave him a tour of the prison. His escort, a stocky, dark-haired man, wore a gray sport coat and white shirt rather than a uniform.

"Call me Jim," the man said, "and take this." He handed George a visitor's ID in a clip-on case. "Wear it on your lapel, and remember that you must be escorted wherever you go." George nodded in agreement.

"Now that we've satisfied the rules, I'll bet you would like some coffee, right?" Jim asked as they entered the prison's interior.

"Yes, thank you." George said.

When they reached the end of the hall, Jim held his ID card up to a small window. "Stappleton with one guest," he said into a small microphone mounted on the wall. A buzzer sounded and they pushed through the door. They walked through a maze of hallways and out into the open.

George found himself in an enclosed courtyard covered with sparse grass and criss-crossed with sidewalks. The boundaries of the courtyard were formed by massive gray walls or by the fronts of buildings. All the windows were barred.

"I thought I'd take you to the RDC area," Jim said. "They have a kitchen there and they make the best coffee in the place."

"What's RDC?" George asked, as they continued to walk across the courtyard.

"That's our Reception and Diagnostic Center. All new inmates report there first. No matter where they're from, even if they're from another institution, we run them through an entire process."

As Jim spoke, they approached a two-story building on the perimeter of the courtyard. The back of the slate-colored building abutted the high wall surrounding the courtyard. "Prisoners arrive through an entrance on the other side of the main wall," Jim explained. "It's the only way in here for these guys."

A security guard standing just inside the door nodded at them as they entered. They made their way down a tiled hallway to a set of heavy glass doors marked RECEPTION AND DIAGNOSTIC CENTER. "Here we are," Jim said. "This is our combination locker room and office."

Jim pushed open one of the doors as a buzzer sounded. As George entered, he noticed several examination tables in the center of the room. On one side of the tables were two shower stalls with plastic curtains. On the other side were two cubicles for changing clothes, separated by a rough wooden bench. A few men, wrapped in towels, sat hunched-over on the bench, staring at the floor, while several men stood around the area in varying stages of undress.

A sliding steel door dominated the far side of the windowless room, topped by a red light.

A man stopped dripping from the nearest shower stall and a guard handed him a towel. "Dry off and lie down over there," he said, pointing to the center examination table. "I'll get your form filled out." The guard walked over to one of the two battered desks standing near the back wall and began to peck away on an old Royal typewriter.

As George and his escort watched the events from the entrance, a man wearing a light blue work shirt with rolled-up sleeves, interrupted their observations. "Jim, how are you?" he asked, apparently oblivious to the convicts watching them. "I haven't seen you over here for some time."

"I'm fine," Jim responded. "George, this is Gary Davidson. He's our resident counselor, in charge of RDC." George and Gary shook hands. To George, Gary looked more like a teacher than a correctional officer. He was in his early 30s, and wore gold-rimmed glasses; his breast pocket was stuffed with pens.

"George is here to talk about inmate education with the Super," Jim explained. "I thought I'd get him some of your good coffee and let him see where the process starts."

"What all do you do in here?" George asked Gary.

"The two guys you just saw walk into the shower stalls over there are getting our first-class treatment: Hot water and de-licing shampoo..." Gary stopped talking as the pager on his belt began beeping incessantly. "Excuse me," he said. He walked to the second desk in the back of the room and spoke on the telephone. He returned minutes later. "What's up?" Jim asked.

"That was the Super's office," Gary said. "As usual, it's good news and bad. The good is that they caught Danny Lee, just before dawn, down in McKinley County."

"Great news," Jim said with obvious relief. "When are they going to return him?"

"Word is that the sheriff doesn't trust putting him in the county jail," Gary answered." He loaded Danny Lee in the back of his car and started driving. They could be here any time."

"What was the bad news?" Jim asked.

"Oh, yeah," Gary said. "There's a message for you, George. This whole scene with Danny Lee means that the Super won't be able to keep his appointment with you today at all. He's meeting with the governor all morning then he has a press conference this afternoon. The message says to convey his apologies."

"Did the message say when he wants to meet?"

"Nope," Gary answered. "You can call his secretary before you leave today."

George nodded and looked back at the convicts he had seen when he entered the building. All of the inmates had finished showering and had been examined. Two guards cuffed each inmate and linked a single chain through their left arms.

The red light over the door began to flash as it slid back. The inmates filed through the opening, accompanied by two of the security officers.

"Who is this Danny Lee guy you've been talking about?" George asked.

"I forgot," Gary said. "You're not from around here. The local; papers have really been working us over about Danny Lee."

"His name," Jim added, "is Danny Lee Gilbert. Twenty-two years ago, he caused a real stir in these parts. He worked for one of the big copper mines in the southern part of the state. Crazy as hell, 23 years old, in trouble all the time. Mostly for mixing booze and whites."

"Right," Gary went on. "Copper was booming then, and the mine didn't shut down for most holidays. Over Thanksgiving, Danny Lee picked up a lot of money working shifts for guys who wanted to take off. He was working shifts for guys who wanted to take off. He was working 16, sometimes 24, hours a day, popping little white pills to keep going.

"The Sunday after Thanksgiving he goes over to his girlfriend's house, wired on speed and carrying a bottle of bourbon. Nobody knows what set him off, but he lost his temper. He and his girlfriend start yelling at each other. She runs outside and he chases after her waiving a .44 in the air. She starts scratching him, so he takes his gun and shoots her—right between the eyes. Then he shoots her three more times.

"Her sister hears the noise and comes around the corner," Gary added. "Danny Lee sees her and shoots her. Then he reloads and runs in the house and finds the sister's nine-year-old daughter, trying to hide in her closet. He shoots her. And then he goes outside and sees the next-door neighbor looking over the wall. So Danny Lee shoots him. "He kills all four of them. Shot each of them four times."

"How'd they catch him?" George asked.

"Danny Lee had an arsenal in his pickup truck," Jim answered. "He would have been tough to bring in. But he was too crazy to drive. On the way out the driveway he ran into a tree. When the sheriff's deputies got there, he was out cold."

"At the trial," Gary continued, "Danny Lee claimed he was crazy when he killed those people. Nobody in a small mining town is going to buy an insanity plea. 'Guilty on four counts of murder one', the jury said."

"The judge sentenced him to die," Jim went on. "But the Supreme Court ruled against the death penalty just before his execution was scheduled. So he was resentenced. Four life sentences one after the other. People figured he'd never get out."

"They put him in the state pen," Gary explained. "Maximum security. And Danny Lee settles in and doesn't bother anybody. Eighteen years he's quiet, respectful, and reliable."

"They transfer him here," Jim added, "to medium security And Danny Lee responds real well. He's totally

straight, polite, and every now and then he turns a bit of info for the officers."

"So we made him a trustee," Gary said. "And he gets to work on some building projects around the prison. He does good work, works extra hours without complaining."

"As a reward," Jim said bitterly, "he gets put on 'work release'. That means we drive him into town and drop him at a street corner and let him stand there until this contractor picks him up in his truck and drives him out to a construction site. And that evening the contractor drops him off at the same downtown corner. And we pick him up and bring him back here."

"Is that the usual treatment?" George asked. "I don't see how you can let a guy like that out on the streets."

"It depends on what you mean by 'a guy like that'," Gary responded. "I know it sounds irresponsible. And it would be, too, if we gave those privileges to the same guy as when he was first arrested. But you've got to remember the effect of all those years. We had 22 years to look at Danny Lee. All the evidence we had available said that he had really changed, that he wasn't a threat to society anymore. From the administration's point of view, he was a model prisoner, not a dangerous criminal. The situation seems to indicate that we were wrong, but we acted on the best evidence available."

"Anyway," Jim went on, "his work release goes on for about 10 months. Nobody says anything, but I doubt that anybody in the general public knew what was happening. Then, the night before last, he's not there. The guard who was driving the bus figures he's working overtime -- it had happened before—so he waits rather than puts in an alert. The word doesn't get out until almost 9 that night."

"I was surprised when I heard," Gary continued. "I couldn't figure Danny Lee to do something like that. He must know that we're going to reassign him to the pen once we put him back."

"What was he trying to do?" George asked.

"No telling," Jim answered. "The message from the Super's office said they caught him before dawn this morning back where he did the killings. Nobody knows what he planned to do, 'cause he got caught before he could do it. But if you ask me…" Gary's pager interrupted him. Gary hurried back to his desk.

He returned a moment later. "We've got to get ready. They're bringing Danny Lee in now—be here in two minutes. The sheriff's car just came through the main gate."

"George," Jim said, "This building is secured; you won't be able to leave until after this is over. We'll stand back here out of the way. Security will be heavy for a bit, but as long as you're with me, it will be OK for you to watch. Whatever happens, don't interfere or say anything."

Suddenly, the light above the entrance door began to flash and a buzzer sounded. Six guards entered the room; one stood in each corner and two framed the door.

Gary went to the door and unlocked its sliding bolts. The door rolled to the side on its tracks and a large

uniformed man entered the room. He wore a glossy Sam Browne gun belt that held a long-barreled revolver. On his head was a large, white cowboy hat with a badge pinned to the band. He looked down at Gary, then around the room with a broad but sardonic smile. Finally, he spoke.

"Well, here he is." The lawman stepped to one side as a man came hurtling through the door. He stumbled as he entered and fell, unable to break his fall with his chained hands. His face hit the floor.

"You all know me," the uniformed man said, "Sheriff Conklin. I'm the guy that gets to mop up after your mistakes. How'd he get so lucky to have guys like you watchin' him?—that's what I want to know."

Gary did not respond. Instead, he went over and helped the chained man to his feet. "You know the procedures, Danny Lee," he said without inflection. "Shower first."

George was unprepared for the real Danny Lee. The convict was small—probably no more than 5'5"—and wiry. The top of his head was almost entirely bald, but he wore the remaining fringe of hair very long, so that it reached to his collar. George noticed cuts and bruises on the man's bald head.

"Where'd he get those bruises?" Gary asked the sheriff.

"Must've got 'em while he was out," the sheriff said. "They sure didn't happen while he was in my custody."

Gary looked closely at Danny Lee's face, giving special attention to a raw bruise under the convict's left eye. "Sheriff," Gary continued, "You know the regulations on physically abusing prisoners. It sure looks like someone worked him over."

"It wasn't me or any of my men," the sheriff said defensively. "But even if somebody did, it's better'n treating him like an honored guest like y'all do."

"No it's not," Gary said firmly. "You're not hired to administer punishment. The very courts you say you represent would convict you if I could prove what I know happened to this man.

"I can understand your personal feelings, and I sympathize with you. But that badge you're wearing doesn't allow you to take those feelings out on anybody."

"I'm sure you learn that kind of stuff in college," the sheriff shot back. "But you come down to my county, you'll meet 16 people who still cry themselves to sleep every night because of what this guy did." The sheriff punctuated his comment by pushing Danny Lee forward. The convict stumbled in his shackles momentarily then regained his balance. "He gets out again," the sheriff continued, "a lot of people are gonna wonder if you folks can do the job at all. We may have to do something on our own if he gets down our way again."

"What do you plan to do, Sheriff," Gary challenged, "hang him from the old oak tree? Come on. You have a right to those feelings, but you don't have a right to act on them.

"I know you represent your people," Gary continued, "and I know the kind of feelings people have about their neighbors. But, damn it, you stand for something more

than feelings. You represent the law, even in times and places where no one wants to hear about it."

"Hey, look," the sheriff protested, "a little shove now and then doesn't hurt him much, and you guys just want to baby him. Someone's got to make him hurt."

"We don't see things eye-to-eye, Sheriff," Gary concluded. "You do your job. Let me do mine. Just remove the shackles and we'll take over."

Sheriff Conklin chose a key from the ring on his belt and bent over to unlock the shackle on Danny Lee's right ankle. "You know procedure, Sheriff," Gary snapped, "do it right. Sit him down in that chair. I don't want you or Danny Lee getting hurt."

"Whatever you say," the sheriff responded sarcastically. He seized Danny Lee's arm and half led, half dragged him to the chair.

"Sit down, pop," the sheriff growled, "and don't move a muscle." He knelt by the prisoner's right leg, inserted the shackle key, and unfastened the iron shackle. He slid the ring of metal under the chair to Danny Lee's left ankle and moved behind the chair. He knelt to undo the left shackle then stood to unlock the wrist manacles.

"Straighten up there," he snapped, then wrested the chains from Danny Lee's body. "Here's your boy," the sheriff said to Gary. "See if you can keep him this time. He's in deep trouble if he comes back to my county—ever."

Danny Lee pulled free of the sheriff's grasp. "Man, I'm

glad somebody's on my side," he said, extending his hand to Gary.

"Just move over there, Danny Lee," Gary said, pointedly ignoring the outstretched hand. "I don't know why you took off, but you blew it. I'm not on your side, and I don't think anybody in the prison administration will be."

"Wait a minute..." Danny Lee began, but Gary interrupted him.

"No, you want a minute!" Gary answered coldly. "You knew the rules before you took off. They're easy to understand. And you broke 'em, and that's all there is to that.

"But in the process, you broke a lot more. You broke the trust you had developed over the years up at the pen and here. You let all of us down, and you let yourself down. You made us look like fools, and you've made it that much harder for every con in here to try and play it straight."

"Yeah, but you don't understand, man..." Danny Lee pleaded. Gary interrupted again.

"Right now, I'm not inclined to try. You blew it, man, just plain blew it. I want you to know that I feel just as angry as Sheriff Conklin and his men. I won't take that anger out on you, but I am going to be sure you take the consequences for what you did.

"The heat starts now. First, you'll lose your privileges, all of them. You're looking at three or four weeks of solitary. After that, you'll be tried for escape. You can forget about

walking around enjoying yourself like you've been doing. Things have changed, man, and you changed them."

"But you gotta listen to me," Danny Lee protested. "I had a good reason for what I did, damn it, and you don't even want to hear about it."

"You can talk about your reasons in your counseling sessions," Gary responded. "The hammers are going to fall around here. Nothing personal—and I mean that—but things are going to be tough, tough on you, and you've got yourself to thank."

"Shit," Danny Lee said, glaring at the floor "no breaks at all, right?"

"You got that part right," Gary said, "no breaks at all. Just hard time."

"Guess I'm gonna be here a long time," Danny Lee said to Gary as he moved to the examination area. "But you aren't going anywhere neither. I'll wait my chance."

"I'm glad to see that you don't side with this murdering son of a bitch," Sheriff Conklin said, shaking Gary's hand. "But you gotta use more than words to get the attention of a guy like that."

"Maybe so," Gary said as he walked the sheriff to the door, "but according to the law, it's all we've got." The door slid shut as the sheriff eased into the passenger seat of the county car.

The Lesson

"Talk about living between a rock and a hard place, Mike exclaimed.

"Couldn't have put it better myself," George said with a smile. "Nothing short of whips and chains will satisfy the sheriff. But a corrections officer like Gary can't act, even for a moment, like he goes along with what Danny Lee did.

"See, most corrections officers share more feelings with the sheriff than they ever can admit. They have to try all the time not to let themselves get personally involved with the crimes some of their inmates have committed casually.

"There's no easy way to take a stand in this," George went on. "Anytime we talk about punishment, we take on the oldest problem that society has faced—what do you do with people who don't play by the rules? People like Danny Lee have to be punished—not abused, but punished. Those correctional officers are there to administer that punishment."

"I suppose that's true," Mike said. "But the problem is particularly difficult because nobody's very sure why we have prisons. They were invented as a place to keep people who were waiting to be punished, not as the punishment.

"Back in the Middle Ages, the worst punishment imaginable was to be thrown in the dungeon and forgotten, even by the man who sent you there. I've read

lots of old letters by knights in prison, pleading with the King to punish them and let them go."

As they talked, they crossed the state line into New Mexico. "But," Mike went on, "how does Verbal Judo apply to this definition of punishment?"

"Think of it this way. When people break certain rules, they must be punished. That's true whether we're talking about our kids when they consciously violate clearly stated rules, or our employees who disobey a clearly-stated organizational policy, or criminals like that guy we saw at the rest area.

"When someone breaks the rules, people who live according to the rules get angry. It's unavoidable. Once we get angry, we're tempted to take our anger out on the rule-breaker."

"By 'taking it out' on the other person," Mike asked, "Do you mean a physical attack?"

"I hope we're past corporal punishment in any form. It's a violation of the Constitution to strike an imprisoned murderer. I take that to mean we don't believe in physical punishment under any circumstances, even in the home.

"But verbal abuse can be even more devastating than a physical assault. We can avoid hurting the person we punish only be controlling our anger.

"The whole point of Verbal Judo is control. We aren't supposed to hurt people with our words, even if we feel very angry and very hurt, and want to insult and humiliate that person. We stay in control and use our words for a purpose."

"Don't people need to say how and what they feel?" Mike asked. "Sometimes we need to let others know how much they've hurt us."

"I'm not arguing for bottling up feelings," George responded. "But I am saying that certain roles require that we control our desire to say angry words, and those roles include being a good parent, a good manager, or a good corrections officer, among others.

"The difference is between punishing someone as opposed to hurting someone."

"You keep making comparisons between the penal system and family or professional relationships. Are they the same?"

"No, but they have similarities," George replied. "Most parents and managers would do a better job if they'd try to understand the perspective of the correctional officer. See, corrections officers don't decide on the punishment, they administer it. That prevents arbitrary punishment.

"Parents and managers act arbitrarily when they punish their children or employees for irritating or disappointing them. But the lesson from the corrections officer is that punishment must be a clearly defined consequence of precisely identified actions."

"If judo is the 'gentle way'," Mike protested, "how can it be used as a tactic for punishment?"

"Remember that few people ever feel that they deserve to be punished," George answered. "Concepts like 'fair' or fitting' won't make any impact on them.

"But you can demonstrate the fairness of the punishment through disinterest and control, the principles of Verbal Judo. However 'hard' you must be, you never act to hurt.

"The throw that comes closest to that idea in physical judo is tai otoshi. It's sometimes called the 'body-drop throw', and it's one of the most powerful and final throws in judo. Whoever performs it usually wins."

"It sounds like a pro wrestling maneuver," Mike joked. "How does it work?"

"I usually use this throw when my opponent has been using dirty tricks. I want to teach him a lesson, but I don't want to actually hurt him. Unlike most judo moves, I don't have to wait for him to move, and then react. When we're face to face, I reach out and grab his collar with my right hand and his elbow with my left. Then I do a few quick steps.

"First, I step forward and across with my right leg. Then I swing my left foot behind me and plant it in line with my opponent's left foot. Then I step to the right with my right leg across his right shin, so that the surface of my right knee is flush against the opponent's right shin. At this point, just before the throw, I'm in a low stance, pulling with my left arm and pushing with my right.

"I execute the throw by snapping my right leg against the opponent's shin and pulling him forward and downward. He snaps up into the air and comes over hard."

"It sounds like you generate a lot of force that way," Mike said.

"You do. Anyone thrown by tai otoshi remembers it and tries hard to guard against a repeat. It's the closest thing I know of in judo to an implacable force."

"You seem to use it for punishment yourself," Mike said.

"Well, remember that I'm in a physical contest that my opponent entered of his own free will. In that context, it is punishing. I don't know another throw that so convinces my opponent of my control and ability. The impact of the throw is memorable, but when that's combined with obvious skill and control, it is truly intimidating."

"Do you think punishment always needs that element of intimidation?" Mike asked.

"I don't know about 'always'," George responded. "But if you want the punishment to have any deterrent value, I think you need it."

"Can we state this as a principle of Verbal Judo?" Mike asked.

"I think so," George answered.

Be disinterested when you punish.

"That's eight principles," Mike observed. "Are there more?"

"Maybe," George responded, "but not this trip. We're almost home." The eastern horizon glowed with the lights of Albuquerque. "Let's figure out if we need more during the next few days."

10

The Gentle Way of Words

The Principles of Verbal Judo Can Be Used by Everyone

Five months after returning from Las Vegas, George and Mike sat opposite their editor—Helen—at a conference table cluttered with piles of print-outs, bulging manila folders, and page proofs.

"Well, gentlemen," she began, "I must say that I've enjoyed working with you. I feel that we've been able to solve the structural and stylistic problems I pointed out, and you've tightened the exposition nicely. The narratives are now very engaging, and the dialogue is realistic and well-paced."

"If I can speak for both of us," Mike began, "we'd like to thank you for your help. Your comments are especially gratifying because we've put a lot of ourselves into writing these accounts. But unless I'm mistaken, I hear some qualifications coming. Am I right?"

Helen smiled and nodded in agreement. "During these past few months, I've tried to be an advocate for the reader, not a critic of the writers.

"But," she went on, "as we approach publication, I must confess to some serious reservations about the book, which I'd like to address. For one thing, I'm concerned about identifying the readership for this book. And, quite frankly, I'm troubled by some of the unstated implications of Verbal Judo."

"Fine," Mike said patiently, "let's talk about those concerns."

"Right," George insisted. "Explain your 'reservations' about the readership."

"Think of it from a reader's point of view," she replied. "A police officer would undoubtedly find the chapter on enforcement extremely realistic and interesting. A teacher would learn a great deal from your study of motivation. And a salesperson would certainly like your analysis of persuasion.

"But this is an age of specialization. Who would want to read all of these chapters? Will any professional find all of them useful?"

"Certainly," George said firmly. "Even though our narratives consider the principles one at a time; verbal encounters don't sort themselves out so simply. You have to get beyond a 'one encounter, one principle' perspective. Most real-life encounters tend to move in steps through several principles. Some even go through all eight stages before a resolution is achieved."

"You seem to be suggesting some real flexibility for these techniques," Helen remarked.

"Absolutely," George replied. "Just think about the verbal encounters you've found yourself in at home or the office. How many times have you begun by trying to guide or motivate and ended up having to reassure or even enforce?"

"More often than I'd like to recall," she answered, smiling.

"That's really what I'm getting at," George continued. "The problem many people have interacting with others begins with their own lack of flexibility; they don't respond to the changing nature of a verbal exchange.

"Parents, for example, who try to guide or direct their children often find increasing resistance from them. The adult will then often move to the language of enforcement or punishment without realizing that when their purposes change, so must their principles of communication. And when the principle changes the language also has to change. If it doesn't, all kinds of misunderstanding and resentment result."

"I can see that," Helen said. "But are you suggesting that such change and flexibility applies to other encounters?"

"I certainly am," George answered. "Professionals in all walks of life must play numerous roles that depend on the situation and the person they confront. When I was a police officer, I often found myself moving from one principle to another, sometimes through all eight, in a single shift."

"In what way?" Helen asked.

"Police officers probably use the language of enforcement most of the time. But they also have to be ready to use the language of reassurance, or the language of direction or the language of persuasion, or any of the other languages. To be effective, professionals have to possess diverse and flexible linguistic skills."

"Right," Mike insisted. "I think that the very specialization in modern professions that you're talking about, Helen is a serious problem—a problem this book address. I agree, for example, that salespeople can learn from the persuasion chapter, but I also think other readers can as well. I work with lots of government scientists who don't know how to persuade their funders of the value of their research. They can use that principle even more than salespeople can."

"That's true," George added. "The person who has real trouble is the one who stays with only one language and one principle, even when the encounter shifts to a new and different level. The skill of strategic communication lies in the ability to sense when such shifts are taking place. When those changes occur, you have to become who you must in order to handle the encounter with skill and sensitivity. That's professionalism."

"Rhetoric is pretty much a lost art," Mike went on, "except among those academics who study rather than practice. But the goal of rhetoric from its first development has been to show us ways to adapt our language to our purpose. And that's what these chapters do. They give people a way to define a situation and to respond to their definition with a tactic."

"That's an interesting point," Helen remarked. "You may know that the word 'define' originally meant 'to limit' something."

"Right," George agreed. "When you limit an event, you can control it. And Verbal Judo is a way to control the events in personal encounters."

"That seems valid," Helen acknowledged, "We'll need to make that perspective a little more explicit in our descriptions of the book.

"However," she continued, "Your explanation reinforces my concerns about the other issues here."

"What are they?" George asked, bristling slightly.

"I guess I have the same concern that people expressed in ancient Athens about the first rhetoricians—the sophists. The various chapters may encourage people to misrepresent themselves and their feelings. You seem to argue that people should calculate every statement rather than express what they feel. This book could be read as an apology for the phony—or worse, for the confidence man. I don't feel we want to countenance misrepresentation."

"I respect your concerns," Mike responded, "and I want to assure you that we aren't encouraging manipulative techniques. As I see it, a phony is someone who calculates his statements so we'll believe he's something he's not. Even worse, a confidence man calculates his statements to persuade us to do things he wouldn't do himself. Both of them might use some Verbal Judo tactics, but they ignore the principles."

"And you can't ignore those principles," George broke in. "The key to Verbal Judo is like Dr. Kano's maxim of Jiko no kansei—'You must always strive to perfect others even while perfecting yourself.'

"That point is stressed in the third chapter. It insists that the role you play, or the voice you assume, must enable others to improve themselves. The book always denies manipulative actions—acting to harm someone else or to promote your own selfish intent. The point we try to make throughout the book is that we will communicate more successfully if we comprehend the other's context and point of view rather than insist on our own."

"Absolutely," Mike continued. "Out of necessity, we often have to play out roles in our daily public lives. We're not supposed to express our feelings; we're obligated to make a positive impact on the behavior of others. George is right about these principles being the justification behind Verbal Judo."

"You're very persuasive on this issue," Helen said thoughtfully. "But you should also be aware that you're addressing a highly sensitive area. Do you really want people to deny their feelings? A book by Arlie Russell Hochschild called The Manged Heart talks about the 'commercialization of human feeling'. The author says that corporations increasingly demand simulated emotions from their employees.

"Such demands place real psychological burdens on people—especially people like flight attendants and others who serve the public. They have to endure a lot of rude behavior from customers. Your book seems to advocate simulated emotions, and I worry that your advice would increase the burden placed on such employees."

"I think we'd both agree with you that 'contact professionals' have a difficult role to perform," George said. "And when they work in private industry, the difficulty increases because 'the customer is always right'."

Mike nodded in agreement then went on. "But I think the principles of Verbal Judo actually reduce the emotional burden on contact professionals. Verbal Judo gives them a positive alternative to venting their anger at a rude customer and to masking their emotions with phony smiles."

"You see," George continued, "we recommend that people try to achieve disinterest, a state in which they don't prejudge others or allow their own biases to interfere with their ability to listen and respond to others. We remain open and flexible, ready to respond rather than react."

"Exactly," Mike said with a vigorous nod. "In many ways, it is good for people to get some 'distance' from their personal feelings when they deal with people unlike themselves. And that's particularly true in professional or business settings."

"I'm not sure I agree with that generalization," Helen replied.

"Let me give you an example," George went on. "I once was asked to counsel a state police officer who had a bad record—several charges of excessive force and a large number of 'resist arrests'.

"I asked him to explain his record. He told me that every time someone shook a fist at him or insulted him, his face would turn bright red, like a boiled lobster.

"He blamed that physiological reaction for his trouble. Once the subject saw that he could upset the trooper, he'd try to up the ante, to manipulate the officer's feelings until he lost control and his professional credibility."

"I've met people like that officer," Helen said. "They seem to be victims of their emotions."

"That's how he felt," George continued. "When I asked what made him turn red, he explained that some inner voice told him 'you don't have to take that crap'. The tension between the suspect's words and his inner voice upped his blood pressure.

"Now this man was a good officer in other situations, and worth keeping on the force, so I asked him about some self-defense principles. 'Who would you rather fight with,' I asked him, 'a guy who comes at you with his arms flailing or somebody who steps back into a defensive posture and quietly challenges you to take him'?"

"I don't know self-defense tactics," Helen said, "but I know which man is more dangerous."

"That's what this trooper concluded. 'Being out of control makes you weak and vulnerable to someone who knows what he's doing,' he said. And we agreed that strength comes from staying calm when others lose control.

"He recognized that his real problem was his tension. It made him egotistical and self-centered. He acted according to his feelings in rigid, inflexible ways that made him incapable of responding skillfully or professionally.

"And that's why we recommend that people get some distance from their feelings. When others become upset, we must stay open and flexible in order to help or control them. We really can't express our own feelings."

"I think I see what you mean," Helen responded. "Since we can't avoid many stressful situations, Verbal Judo can at least give us some measure of personal control. And that self-control may allow us to control the situation.

"I'm satisfied with that answer," she continued. "But one of my concerns is still unresolved."

"Tell us," George said.

"The encounters you describe all reach satisfactory conclusions without any real emotional content. But many of the conflicts we have to face are charged with personal feelings. It seems to me that the tactics you call Verbal Judo oversimplify the complexity of long-term human relationships."

"I don't think we're talking about deep, emotionally charged relationships," Mike answered. "Verbal Judo is a rhetorical technique. It isn't intended for intimate relationships; it is only a means to change behavior.

"In dealing with someone we care deeply about, we have to move beyond behavior alone. We have to make considerable efforts to know the other person's thought processes, the ways they respond to ideas and react to new situations. We need to learn what they're like so that

we can anticipate their needs rather than respond to the behavior."

"I agree," George said. "I feel that Verbal Judo is best suited to 'situational rhetoric', language for the immediate moment: the unplanned confrontation, the encounter that abruptly begins to move in unpredictable ways, the sudden discovery that the person you are speaking to is very different from you.

"In such situations, you must apply rhetorical strategies. You have to keep control of your own perspective and attempt to read your audience. Then you try to fashion a voice that will carry your point to that audience. And you have to organize your verbal exchange so that you accomplish a clearly defined purpose.

"Each situation is unique even though some of the elements may be typical of other encounters. We have to notice the unique elements and be flexible enough to respond to them using the kind of perspective described above.

"Verbal Judo offers predictable tactics and strategies enabling us to relate to others effectively under the most sudden and trying circumstances. It prepares us to act with control and intelligence even when we face the most explosive or unexpected situations."

"Then Verbal Judo does reinterpret the principles of physical judo," Helen concluded. "Didn't Dr. Kano make a distinction between the 'lesser' judo and the 'greater' judo?"

"Yes," George answered. "The lesser judo, according to Dr. Kano, is the physical form of Judo. The greater judo observes the three maxims discussed in the book. The first tells us to strive for perfection as human beings. The second insists that we consider the welfare and benefit of others. And the third maxim is the key to accomplishing the first two—maximum efficiency with minimum effort."

"I guess we've come back to Dr. Akiyama's discovery," Helen added. "By yielding we gain control; through gentleness we become strong."

The three sat silently, sharing their agreement. Then Mike spoke: "Let's conclude by reviewing the maxims of Verbal Judo in the light of Dr. Kano's principles."

VERBAL
JUDO

Move confrontations away from conclusions back to the reasoning process

When you must guide others to a wiser course of action, help them seek new approaches rather than argue about the right answer. Never debate any point that can be resolved by examining the facts.

Motivate others by raising their expectations of themselves. When you seek to motivate others, begin by discovering what they do well. Encourage them to develop their special talents by helping them define their own self-worth.

Persuade others with their energy, not your own

When you wish to convince others, first learn what is in their best interests. Persuade them through an appeal to that interest, not through the force of your words.

Direct others rather than control them

When you supervise others' efforts, recognize their need for independence. Assume responsibility for their doing well, not for doing their job yourself.

Give way in order to control

When negotiating with others who demand that you give in, first seek a middle position that will satisfy their needs and your limits. Insist on discussing principles, not personal preferences.

Embrace frustration with empathy

When you must calm others who are distraught, always harmonize with their pain. Lead them through their distress with reason.

Overcome hard with soft

When you must compel others to obey the law or regulations, ignore the impact of their insults. Enforce the authority of the Institution you represent, not the power of your anger.

Be disinterested when you punish

When you must punish others for violating clearly defined rules, always set aside your personal indignation. Respect the authority the authority than empowers you to discipline.

15235951R00106

Made in the USA
Middletown, DE
31 October 2014